THE TRANSCRIPTS

CHINESE SAYINGS
BOOK 2

LASZLO MONTGOMERY

Chinese Sayings Book 2

By Laszlo Montgomery

Trade Paper: 978-988-8904-06-8
Digital: 978-988-8904-04-4

© 2024 Laszlo Montgomery

HISTORY / Asia / China

EB238

All rights reserved. No part of this book may be reproduced in material form, by any means, whether graphic, electronic, mechanical or other, including photocopying or information storage, in whole or in part. May not be used to prepare other publications without written permission from the publisher except in the case of brief quotations embodied in critical articles or reviews. For information contact info@earnshawbooks.com

Published in Hong Kong by Earnshaw Books Ltd.

CONTENTS

Author's Foreword — IX

Episode 1 Payback! — 1
感恩图报—Gǎn Ēn Tú Bào

Episode 2 Can't Get it out of My Head — 7
余音绕梁—Yú Yīn Rào Liáng

Episode 3 Stop Wasting Time — 13
对牛弹琴—Duì Niú Tán Qín

Episode 4 I Love You Man! — 19
高山流水—Gāo Shān Liú Shuǐ

Episode 5 Give it All You Got! — 25
一鼓作气—Yī Gǔ Zuò Qì

Episode 6 You Smell That? — 31
不知肉味—Bù Zhī Ròu Wèi

Episode 7 Seeing is believing — 37
百闻不如一见—Bǎi Wén Bùrú Yī Jiàn

Episode 8 There's always a way — 43
有志者事竟成（有志竟成）—Yǒu zhì zhě shì jìng chéng

Episode 9 Always expect the unexpected — 49
万事俱备，只欠东风—Wàn Shì Jùbèi Zhǐ Qiàn Dōngfēng

Episode 10 Waiting in Vain — 55
守株待兔—Shǒu Zhū Dài Tù

Episode 11 Showing Paul how to write a song   61
班门弄斧—Bān Mén Nòng Fǔ

Episode 12 Nobody Loves You When You're Down and Out   67
门可罗雀—Mén Kě Luó Què

Episode 13 Knock Knock Knockin' on Heaven's Door   73
釜底游魚—Fǔ Dǐ Yóu Yú

Episode 14 Mr. Good Good   83
好好先生—Hǎo Hǎo Xiānshēng

Episode 15 It's Too Late Baby!   89
病入膏肓—Bìng Rù Gāo Huāng

Episode 16 Be All that You Can Be   97
投笔从戎—Tóu Bǐ Cóng Róng

Episode 17 Makes no difference   105
九牛一毛—Jiǔ Niú Yī Máo

Episode 18 Darn Mulberry Tree!   113
指桑骂槐—Zhǐ Sāng Mà Huái

Episode 19 The Great Rejuvenation   123
多难兴邦—Duō Nàn Xīng Bāng

Episode 20 As close as Lips n' Teeth   131
唇亡齿寒—Chún Wáng Chǐ Hán

Episode 21 I want you to show me the way   141
老马识途—Lǎo Mǎ Shí Tú

Episode 22 Gimme Three Steps   149
退避三舍—Tuì Bì Sān Shè

Episode 23 Run For Your Life	157
项庄舞剑,意在沛公—Xiàng Zhuāng Wǔjiàn, Yìzài Pèigōng	
Episode 24 Looks can be deceiving	171
华而不实—Huá Ér Bù Shí	
Episode 25 Help!	177
涸辙之鲋—Hé Zhé Zhī Fù	
Episode 26 Let's Stick Together	183
物以类聚—Wù Yǐ Lèi Jù	
Episode 27 Why Can't We Live Together?	191
势不两立—Shì Bù Liǎng Lì	
Episode 28 Please Allow Me to Introduce Myself	199
毛遂自荐—Máo Suì Zì Jiàn	
Episode 29 Be like Kong Rong	207
孔融让梨—Kǒng Róng Ràng Lí	
Episode 30 Owned!	213
骄兵必败—Jiāo Bīng Bì Bài	
Episode 31 First Strike	219
先发制人—Xiān Fā Zhì Rén	

AUTHOR'S FOREWORD

I'm thrilled to present to you the second in a series of three books containing Chinese "chengyu" idioms.

Like the Chinese Sayings in Book 1 of the series, these are all derived from ancient and medieval classical literature, and stories rooted in history. Even though many of them are more than two thousand years old, they are still widely used in modern Chinese to convey something on the one hand complex but on the other hand somewhat profound. They are concise yet memorable.

One of the aspects of these Chinese Sayings is that their figurative meaning almost always could not be deduced simply by reading the four (or more) characters.

About five years after I launched the China History Podcast I thought that with these "chengyu" phrases so often rooted in history, why not launch a new podcast show that would introduce one chengyu per episode, whatever the origins of the idiom, be it a work of literature, folklore, official history, historical events, or philosophical text.

What's cool about these chengyu or Chinese Sayings is that they convey rich meanings, morals, and pearls of wisdom in a compact form, often summarizing a story or a moral lesson. Chengyu phrases add depth and nuance to the language.

Since I launched the Chinese Sayings Podcast, over 90 episodes have been produced as of late 2024. Both Cathay Pacific and Singapore Airlines carry these Chinese Sayings Podcast shows in their inflight entertainment systems.

In these anthologies being published by Earnshaw Books, the entirety of these famous and historic Chinese Sayings is being presented in three volumes. Each consists of my curated selections of the most engaging, relatable, and thought-provoking Chengyu-Chinese Sayings. No matter if you're a fluent Chinese speaker, in the process of learning or have never studied before, these books introduce you to a wonderful slice of Chinese culture that you can use in your daily life, at home, at the office, or out with your friends and family.

Here in Volume 2 of this 3-Part Chinese Sayings Anthology, chengyu idioms from the Warring States and Han Dynasty are featured. I hope you will enjoy and appreciate these cultural classics from more than two thousand years ago.

Laszlo Montgomery

 Chinese Sayings Book 2
Episode 1

THE TRANSCRIPTS

PAYBACK!

感恩图报—Gǎn Ēn Tú Bào

TRANSCRIPT

00:00 Greetings everyone all over the world, this is Laszlo Montgomery again with another nice Chinese Saying for you. This one today is something that highlights one of the many traditional virtues of Chinese culture. I feel the same way about this particular virtue and so do a lot of other people in other cultures as well.

00:20 There's an old Chinese saying that, I'm paraphrasing so as not to dump a whole lot of Chinese on you, that says, the favor of a drop of water should be returned with an entire fount of water. You know, someone does you a good turn, you should return the favor and even more so, to show your appreciation. One good turn deserves another, I guess you can say.

00:39 And the Chinese saying we're going to look at today is all about this very idea. Today we look at Gǎn Ēn Tú Bào.

00:48 Okay, as we always do here at the Chinese Sayings Podcast, let's lay this one down on the dissecting table

CHINESE SAYINGS BOOK 2
EPISODE 1

and pick it apart.

00:56 Gǎn means to thank or to appreciate. Ēn means grace, kindness, a favor or help. Gǎn Ēn, appreciate or be thankful for the kindness, appreciate the favor. Tú in this example means to intend to do something, to plan to. And Bào means to pay back or reciprocate. Tú Bào to intend to reciprocate or pay back. Then we daisy chain the whole thing together and get Thankful Favor Intend to Pay Back.

01:31 Okay, that's easy to figure out. We can see where this one is heading. But what's the story behind that? That's the raison d'être of this podcast program. How did those four characters get strung together like that? I don't mean to call anyone Shirley, but surely there's a story behind this one.

01:53 And wouldn't you know it, our story today once again comes from the venerable Shǐ Jì 史记, the Records of the Grand Historian. Sīmǎ Qiān's blockbuster from the Hàn dynasty. Contained in this classic is a story about someone we covered once in the China History Podcast episode 111 on the history of the once mighty Wú State.

02:19 Our star today is a famous name from the Spring and Autumn Period, that the portion of the Eastern Zhōu that came before the Warring States Period. This Chūnqiū 春秋 or Spring and Autumn era was the time of Lǎozǐ and Confucius and many other great Chinese philosophers. Today we look at a story that co-stars the great general, strategist, personal friend of Sūnzǐ, a.k.a. Sun Tzu as we

2

CHINESE SAYINGS BOOK 2
EPISODE 1

say here in Hollywood, and a model for what it means to be loyal, Wǔ Zǐxū 伍子胥.

02:52 Wǔ Zǐxū and his mighty Wú army were planning an attack on the state of Zhèng to the north, near Luòyáng. Zhèng was a Zhou Dynasty vassal state that had seen better days. Now under their King Dìng of Zheng, Zhèng Dìng Gōng 郑定公, who reigned 529-514BCE, they were vulnerable and in the gunsights of the Wú State.

03:15 As Wǔ Zǐxū readied his army to march north and take down Zhèng, King Dìng called out to all his generals, officials and people and offered great rewards for anyone who could come up with a plan to defend against and ultimately defeat Wú. Four days passed and no one could offer King Dìng any advice on how to handle the coming onslaught from Wǔ Zǐxū's great Wú army.

03:43 King Dìng started to sweat as Wǔ Zǐxū's army began its march north to do battle. At this most desperate hour, a simple fisherman walked to the palace. In his hand he carried an oar from his fishing boat, a boat he inherited from his father, another fisherman. The king and his officials looked at the young fisherman skeptically but heard him out. When he asked the fisherman how many chariots, soldiers and weapons he needed, the fisherman replied, "I need nothing from you. I will deal with Wǔ Zǐxū's army by myself and with this single oar in my hand."

04:22 The king and his officials passed a few one liners back and forth and had a little fun with this young sincere

CHINESE SAYINGS BOOK 2
EPISODE 1

fisherman who stood before them. "Okay young man, go then. Go stop this terrible army from advancing on our kingdom and you shall be amply rewarded." The king and his ministers had sadly concluded that desperate times required desperate measures. And these were desperate times. They had nothing to lose from this Hail Mary.

04:49 The fisherman thereupon, with oar in hand, began walking slowly southward to meet up with Wŭ Zĭxū's army. He came upon the military camp, took a big breath, gathered up his courage and began walking into the center of the military camp. He began singing a song loudly, "Man hiding amongst the reeds! Man hiding amongst the reeds! Remember who saved your life when you were drowning in the river! The Big Dipper carved in your body! Your sword was returned to you! Do you remember the fisherman who saved your life?"

05:28 Wŭ Zĭxū heard this chant from his tent and perked up at once. "Who is that out there?" he demanded. "Bring him to me!" His soldiers led the fisherman into Wŭ Zĭxū's tent and he stood before the mighty general carrying his oar.

05:47 "Why have you come here, young man?" Wŭ Zĭxū asked.

05:52 "Perhaps you recognize this oar, General Wŭ," the young man said. "My father was a fisherman before me and used it for his livelihood. He also once saved your life with this oar." Wŭ Zĭxū was at once brought to tears as he recalled so many years ago when he had almost died trying to get across a river. He had almost drowned

4

CHINESE SAYINGS BOOK 2
EPISODE 1

in this incident but a fisherman had saved him. He had always wanted to find some way to pay the fisherman back for his act of kindness but all these years the chance had never come.

06:25 The fisherman replied, "We people in Zhèng are under attack by you. Our livelihood is being threatened. The king offered a reward to see who could stop your advance. I come here before you and ask you to remember the good deed my father did for you once saving your life."

06:44 Wǔ Zǐxū of course remembered this incident from long ago. The fisherman continued, "I am humbly asking you to consider halting your plans of conquest of Zhèng and leave us be for the sake of the deed my father did for you all those years ago."

07:02 Wǔ Zǐxū said, tears still falling from his eyes, "If not for your father I would have perished that day long ago. I have gone on to live a rich life, attaining high rank. Yet none of this could ever have happened had your father not saved me."

07:20 At once, Wǔ Zǐxū gave the order for the army to begin packing up and to begin marching back to Wú. The campaign to attack Zhèng was ended.

07:30 The fisherman returned to Zhèng and told King Dìng that it was over. Wǔ Zǐxū and the Mighty Wú army were gone. King Dìng could hardly contain his relief and thankfulness at the young fisherman. As promised, he

5

rewarded him with lands and henceforth he became known throughout the land as the officer fisherman.

07:53 So as Sīmǎ Qiān said in his Shǐjì when telling this story from the ancient state of Wú, Wǔ Zǐxū exhibited the act of Gǎn Ēn Tú Bào. He remembered the kindness once showed to him and was determined to repay it one day. And when the fisherman came to Wǔ Zǐxū, the great general showed his appreciation and returned the favor. To have done otherwise would have changed our story, and there's another chengyu hanging out there that describes someone who repays a favor by stabbing you in the back.

08:26 This is a chengyu we can all embrace. Gǎn Ēn Tú Bào everyone. Our chengyu for this episode. One good turn deserves another. If someone does you a solid, hey man, "tu bao." Pay them back through some act of kindness or generosity.

08:44 Okay, that's it for this time everyone. Maybe think about coming back next time. We'll have another saying that you can enjoy and add to your growing collection. So until we meet again, this is Laszlo Montgomery welcoming you as I often do, not in vain I hope, to go check out other shows like the China History Podcast and the Tea History Podcast to name a couple.

09:09 I'm signing off from someplace in Los Angeles County, deep in an underground hermetically sealed secret location. Come join me next time, won't you, for another inspirational episode of The Chinese Sayings Podcast.

Chinese Sayings Book 2 Episode 2

CAN'T GET IT OUT OF MY HEAD

余音绕梁—Yú Yīn Rào Liáng

TRANSCRIPT

00:00 Hello again everyone, Laszlo Montgomery with another chengyu, Chinese idiom or Saying. A quickie today, not a long or involved story. But a useful and relatable one all the same.

00:14 Today we look at the woman with the unforgettable voice, Hán É, who, coincidentally was also from the State of Hán. This ancient state is part of what's today Shanxi and Henan. And guess which period of Chinese history our saying for today originated? Well if you guessed the Spring and Autumn Period, you guessed right. Eastern Zhou Dynasty, again!

00:40 The Hán State was completely surrounded by enemies. During the Warring States Period, they were the first kingdom to go. But our story takes place when they were still around.

00:52 This time around at the Chinese Sayings Podcast we're going to learn about Yú Yīn Rào Liáng, and like all the

7

CHINESE SAYINGS BOOK 2
EPISODE 2

Chinese Sayings we'll look at in this second season this one has something to do with music.

01:07 Let's break it down as we always do. Yú Yīn Rào Liáng.

01:14 The first characters Yú means remaining or surplus, among other things.

01:19 Yīn is sound.

01:23 Rào means to revolve, to coil around and Liáng, besides being a very common surname, means the beam of a roof.

01:32 And Ràoliáng means, of a sound, to reverberate. So, at face value these four characters say remaining sound coils around the roof beam or reverberates. What can that possibly mean? Let's find out.

01:49 Today's story comes out of a work we have not referenced yet, the Lièzǐ 列子. This classic from ancient China, along with the Dào Dé Jīng 道德经 and the Zhuāngzi 庄子, are the three books that make up the Daoism trilogy, the three core books of Daoism. And this chengyu comes from Chapter five of the Lièzǐ. It›s called the Tāng Wèn 汤问.the Questions of Tāng. That's first tone tāng. It means soup, but it's also a surname and in this example is the surname of the Shang Dynasty founder, King Tāng. The Shāng being the oldest dynasty in Chinese history for which we have written records. CHP episodes 15 and 114, if you want to hear more. Just sayin'.

CHINESE SAYINGS BOOK 2
EPISODE 2

02:36 | So from this chapter of the Lièzǐ we have the story of Hán É, who traveled from her home in the Kingdom of Hán to the neighboring kingdom of Qí. Qí is in Shandong province. It's been mentioned before. By the time Hán É arrived at the west gate of the city called the Yōng Mén, she was starving, broke and had run out of food.

02:58 | As I said, Hán É had a beautiful singing voice. She could move people to tears sometimes. Hungry and all, she set herself up outside the city gate in the Qí capital Línzī and began singing for her supper in that amazing voice she had.

03:16 | She had attracted quite a crowd and their jaws just dropped as they beheld the sound of her voice, not to mention her beauty. Their hearts were moved with her songs and by the sheer artistry of what they were hearing. And when she left her spot beside the Yōng Mén to go look for an inn to rest, people still stood by the city gate listening, even though there was nobody there anymore. And for three days it was said, when people stopped outside that spot at Yōng Mén where she sang, it's said the sound of Hán É's unforgettable melodious voice still lingered as if she was still standing there.

03:57 | Meanwhile Hán É didn't have enough cash to get a room at any inn. And on top of that the innkeeper really laid into her and scolded her for her poverty and just gave her a whole attitude because of her empty purse and he told Hán É to beat it.

04:15 | She burst into tears at the hopelessness of her situation

9

CHINESE SAYINGS BOOK 2
EPISODE 2

and for the cold-heartedness of the innkeeper. Those who were close by heard the sound of her weeping and were so overwhelmed with grief and sadness themselves that they too were hit with this ungovernable fit of sobbing. And some people were so moved by Hán É that they couldn't sleep or eat for three days. And so they took pity on her and fed her, gave her strings of cash and begged her to return to the Yōng Mén to sing her songs and make everyone happy and cheerful.

04:49 And that's what she did. And she sang for the people of Qi and the residents there, who, over time, also acquired a reputation for their excellent singing, would say of Hán É, Yú Yīn Rào Liáng, that the sound of Hán É's singing lingered and reverberated among the rafters.

05:09 And there's a rejoinder to this, you know, sort of like in that past episode from last season, Episode three, of a swan feather from a thousand miles away, Qiān lǐ sòng é máo 千里送鹅毛. That chengyu would be followed with the words lí qīng qíngyì zhòng 礼轻情意重. It's a mere trifle but it's heavy with meaning and affection.

05:35 Well, in the case of Hán É not only did the sounds linger among the rafters, but sān rì bù jué 三日不绝 it didn't stop for three days. Sān rì, three days, bùjúe, was prolonged. So that's the complete deluxe version of this chengyu. four characters plus four. But just like Qiān lǐ sòng é máo, all you have to say is Yú Yīn Rào Liáng and you're in like Flynn. The rejoinder no es necesario. If you want the best of both worlds there's also a conjunction of the two that goes Rào Liáng Sān Rì, it reverberated

CHINESE SAYINGS BOOK 2
EPISODE 2

among the rafters. San ri, for three days. But if you just say Yú Yīn Rào Liáng, you're golden. No one is going to look at you funny or call you a jerk.

06:21 Nowadays this chengyu is used to describe what you might say after hearing an incredible speech or after attending a Ted Talk or anything like that and if the words spoken affected you, you know, like words can do sometimes, then you can tell your friend, Yú Yīn Rào Liáng. Wow, the words are still reverberating in my head. So you can use it in that way too. Anything, a speech, a tune, a podcast, whatever. If you can't get that out of your head, you have every right to say Yú Yīn Rào Liáng or any of the other variations of that chengyu.

07:01 And as far as the rejoinder sān rì bù jué, completely optional.

07:07 So that, watashi no yūjin, is gonna to be that for this time. Nothing long and drawn out, a quick simple and easy Chinese Saying with a simple and easy story attached to it. I use this one every now and then. Now you can too. Yú Yīn Rào Liáng.

07:26 If you haven't figured out yet all the Chinese names and words as well as the tone marks on the Pinyin are all available for you at the website to assist you if you need it. That's at Teacup.media.

08:29 This here's Laszlo Montgomery signing off once again from the City of Angels, Jiāzhōu Luòshānjī. Please consider coming back next time, would ya', for another

CHINESE SAYINGS BOOK 2
EPISODE 2

useful, satisfying and nutritious chengyu here at The Chinese Sayings Podcast.

 Chinese Sayings Book 2
Episode 3

STOP WASTING TIME

对牛弹琴—Duì Niú Tán Qín

TRANSCRIPT

00:00 Hey everybody Laszlo Montgomery here, back once again for another nice juicy Chinese Saying to add to your collection. I hope by now you've tried them out here and there and that they've been of some use to you in the course of your daily life.

00:17 Today is another great one, again, one of my personal favorites because this one, I use it all the time. Such is my fate in life.

00:25 Duì Niú Tán Qín

00:29 And to learn where today's chengyu came from, as we always seem to do, we travel back to China's most ancient evenings, not as far back as the Warring States Period this time. But the story behind this Chinese Saying does take place during the Eastern Han which is still pretty far back, a couple thousand years ago.

CHINESE SAYINGS BOOK 2
EPISODE 3

00:48 The source from which this chengyu sprang from was called the Móuzǐ Lǐhuòlùn 牟子理惑论. Not a well-known work but as far as Chinese Buddhist-related classics go it's one of the bigger ones. Master Mou's Treatise on Settling Doubts. Mostly this work is referred to as The Móuzǐ.

01:06 Let's introduce the stars of today's drama. Top billing, no surprise here, goes to Móu Róng 牟融, also know by his nickname of Master Móu or Móuzǐ 眸子. Don't confuse him with another Móu Róng from the Tang Dynasty. Two different people, but same name, strangely enough.

01:24 We're in the early years of the Eastern Han, around the year 50-60, to give you a bit of a time stamp. Móu Róng was a Confucian scholar official who had been an early convert to Buddhism. He knew his Confucian classics and his Buddhist scripture inside out and was particularly good at explaining Buddhism to the uninitiated and what it was all about.

01:47 And this work, the Móuzǐ Lǐhuòlùn, like Plato's Republic, is a dialogue between Móuzǐ and someone, presumably a Confucianist, and all his questions regarding Buddhism are explained.

02:04 Móuzǐ was a master of the Confucian classics and he had his special way of explaining answers to questions that some of his fellow scholars posed to him about Buddhist teachings.

CHINESE SAYINGS BOOK 2
EPISODE 3

02:15 | And with all that info now playing in the background, without further ado, let's look at the four characters of Duì Niú Tán Qín one by one. You'll see with this one you can almost figure out what this one is all about once you hear the meaning of each of the four characters.

02:34 | Duì Niú Tán Qín.

02:36 | Duì in this case means to face or towards.

02:40 | A Niú is a cow or an ox.

02:43 | Tán means, among a few other things, to play, like a musical instrument, one that has strings, a guitar, zither, or piano.

02:53 | And a Qín is a zither-like instrument of China that has seven strings

02:59 | So Duìniú, facing the ox, followed by tán qín which means to play a zither or play a lute. Face Ox Play Lute. Hmmmm, before you jump to any conclusions, let's get to the story which reveals the hidden meaning.

03:18 | Okay, we already know of Móu Róng, a.k.a. Móuzǐ. So one day at the palace of the Han Emperor, his Confucian colleagues hit him up and inquired why it was that every time they asked him about the Buddhist sutras, he always had to start quoting from the Shī Jīng 诗经 or the Shàng Shū 尚书 or some other Confucian classic from the Zhou Dynasty to provide an answer. Can't he just explain it at face value?

15

CHINESE SAYINGS BOOK 2
EPISODE 3

03:44 Móuzǐ said to them, "Look, guys, you have almost no understanding of Buddhism whatsoever. But your grasp of the Confucian classics is second to none. If I start discussing Buddhist sutras with you, I'm spinning my wheels. How are you gonna get what I'm saying? I have to find some medium to convey the meaning to you so that you can have your questions sufficiently answered."

04:10 Móuzǐ continued, "Let me give you an example. Do you remember the musician Gōngmíng Yí 公明仪? He was real big in the Warring States Period. Top qín performer in China. A little eccentric but quite a musician. When he played he brought down the house every time.

04:29 But one day Gōngmíng Yí was out in nature, playing his qín in the fields and completely absorbed in his music. He was doing one of his most famous and inspirational pieces, Qīng Jiáo 清角. Yet it bothered him, why was it that all the cows grazing in the field where he had sat himself down, why were they completely unmoved by his playing? They just stood there completely unaware, chewing their cud and seemingly oblivious to such magnificent sounds emanating from his instrument.

05:02 So Gōngmíng Yí changed things up a little bit and played a few riffs that mimicked the sound of mosquitoes, flies and even the sound of a lowing calf. And then he saw all the cows in the field, every one, their ears waggled, they looked up and started swishing their tails happily, seemingly affected by the musical sounds they were hearing.

CHINESE SAYINGS BOOK 2
EPISODE 3

05:28 | So the Confucian colleagues of Master Móu nodded their heads silently. And Móuzĭ said, "Hey no offense fellas, but if I'm going to give you direct answers from Buddhist scripture, it's like Gōngmíng Yí playing his qín to the cows. He had to find a way to make a connection and that's all I'm doing by bringing in the Chinese classics to explain myself to you."

05:47 | Well these gathered officials mumbled amongst themselves and nodded to Master Móu, but I'm not sure how they felt about this kind of comparison.

05:57 | But the use of this idiom, Duì Niú Tán Qín, quoted from Master Móu›s Treatise on Settling Doubts, the Móuzĭ Lǐhuòlùn, most certainly looks down on the audience and isn't terribly respectful. To imply that what you have to say can't possibly be appreciated by your audience at that time, well, that's a kind of a distant cousin to last week's episode that introduced Qǔ Gāo Hè Guǎ 曲高和寡.

06:25 | This Saying, Duì Niú Tán Qín, is our English version of to cast pearls before swine. It says what you're presenting can't be understood and certainly not appreciated by your audience. To play a lute to a cow. You're wasting your effort.

06:42 | So you can remember this one next time you see someone blathering away in vain about something and the person they're directing this to has no idea what they're talking about. You can tell that person, hey forget it, Duì Niú Tán Qín. You're wasting your time. You're preaching to

CHINESE SAYINGS BOOK 2
EPISODE 3

deaf ears. You're talkin' over their heads. You're playing a lute to a cow. You're casting pearls among swine, as Matthew said.

07:06 So you can keep this one handy for safekeeping. As I said, I must often resort to this one from time to time. Took a bunch of people from China to The Met last year to go see a ballet. When it was all over, one of them asked me what did I think? I answered Duì Niú Tán Qín. I didn't know enough about ballet to appreciate it. The beauty and meaning of this performance was lost on such a Philistine as your humble narrator.

07:35 That is all I have for you this time. Laszlo Montgomery here reminding you to also check out the China History Podcast and the Tea History Podcast over at Teacup. media. That's enough grandstanding for one episode. Take care everyone. I hope to see you again next time for another musical episode of the Chinese Sayings Podcast.

Chinese Sayings Book 2 Episode 4

I LOVE YOU MAN!

高山流水—Gāo Shān Liú Shuǐ

TRANSCRIPT

00:00 Hello again everybody, thanks for tuning in to the Chinese Sayings Podcast. Laszlo Montgomery here with another chengyu...

00:09 And like the past five episodes, I have for all of you another musical Chinese Saying: Gāo Shān Liú Shuǐ, one of the more better known chengyu. But who am I to say? I didn't grow up hearing this one.

00:22 And before we lay this saying down on the dissecting table, let me first say it comes from a source that we've used before. This one comes to us straight from the Lüshi Chunqiu 吕氏春秋, "The Discourses of Lü Buwei".

00:36 If you can remember from way back in Season 1 Episode 2, I told you the story of Tan Xiao Shi Da. How can you forget the Marquis of Shǔ who for the sake of some nice swag invited the Qin State to build the Stone Cattle Road and come down to his perfect little world, down in amazing Sichuan Province with its pandas, tea and

CHINESE SAYINGS BOOK 2
EPISODE 4

	spicy food. And before you knew it, this Shǔ ruler wasn't the ruler any more.
01:05	Same source for this one today. Gāo Shān Liú Shuǐ is not only a famous chengyu, it's also one of the most famous Chinese songs from ancient times. Here's what it means:
01:17	Gāo Shān Liú Shuǐ.
01:21	Gāo means tall, high or lofty.
01:24	Shān is a mountain. Gāo shān, lofty mountains.
01:30	Liú means to flow and Shuǐ means water or in this example Liú Shuǐ, the flowing waters of a river.
01:39	Gāo Shān Liú Shuǐ - Lofty mountains and flowing water. Hmmm, that must mean something so let's get right into the story.
01:49	Well, if this one didn't come from the Warring States Period, then it musta come from the Spring and Autumn period which preceded the Warring States.
01:57	There are two stars getting equal billing in this production. Yú Bóyá and Zhōng Zǐqī. Yú Bóyá, better known perhaps, simply by his given name of Bóyá, was an official from the State of Jìn, stationed next door in Chu, who was also a great musician. And his instrument was the qín, the zither or lute, the same exact instrument from Duì Niú Tán Qín, playing a zither to an ox. How can we forget that one? This story takes place in the state

CHINESE SAYINGS BOOK 2
EPISODE 4

of Chu in the city of Hànyáng 汉阳, today one of the tri-cities that makes up the mighty city of Wuhan. Yú Bóyá was there as an envoy from his home state of Jìn.

02:41 One gorgeous evening under the moonlight Bóyá was out on his boat playing his music and in the distance he espied a rustic woodsman in the forest quietly listening intently. Bóyá at once judged this book by its cover and thought, how can such a rough looking fellow as this who obviously isn't from the city and has no formal education, how can he possibly appreciate his music?

03:09 Bóyá called out to him and asked this guy his name and the man replied Zhōng Zǐqī. Yú Bóyá thought he'd have a little fun at Mr. Zhōng's expense and asked him, "I bet you can't name that tune I just played."

03:22 Without a moment's hesitation Zhōng Zǐqī answered, "Who doesn't know that one? Kǒngzǐ kū Yán Huí, Confucius Crying over the death of Yan Hui." Bóyá was sort of taken aback by such a bucolic looking fellow knowing this, and so he pressed him on the technical aspects of the piece. This man of the woods was able to explain, quite expertly I might add, what this musical work was all about. So Bóyá once again, he was utterly taken aback by Zhōng Zǐqī›s musical knowledge.

03:57 Bóyá said to Zhōng Zǐqī, "How about this one?" And at once he began to play a beautiful tune that he had written that suggested tall mountains.

CHINESE SAYINGS BOOK 2
EPISODE 4

Zhōng Zǐqī closed his eyes and said, "Ahhhh, I can tell right away this one depicts lofty mountains." Yú Bóyá then played a tune that sounded of flowing rivers. Zhōng Zǐqī said, "Swiftly flows the water of the river."

04:25 Bóyá put down his qín and exclaimed, "Dang, I completely misjudged you. You really know my music! I never met someone who has your understanding. You know, people listen to me perform but they just don't get it. But you! You know."

04:43 And the two became fast friends and beside the river they talked on and on about music. Bóyá really believed he had met his soul-mate and these two, Yú Bóyá and Zhōng Zǐqī, right there on the banks of that river, went on to became sworn brothers.

05:00 Furthermore, the two men agreed henceforth every year they would meet at this spot and talk about music and enjoy each other's company.

05:11 A year later to the day, Bóyá was still serving in the State of Chu, and thereupon went to that spot along the river where he had met his sworn brother Zhōng Zǐqī. He got there first and at once began playing. But after a while it became late and no Zhōng Zǐqī. He made inquiries and learned that tragically, Zhōng Zǐqī had, not long ago, died of an illness.

05:40 Yú Bóyá was struck with emotion and such grief that he went to Zhōng Zǐqī›s gravesite and, played Gao Shan Liu Shui one last time. When he finished, with his tears

CHINESE SAYINGS BOOK 2
EPISODE 4

flowing, he took his zither in his hands and smashed it on the rocks that lined the riverbank, vowing that never again would he play his music. The only one who truly understood him and all its meaning and subtleties of his musicianship was now gone from his life. He never picked up an instrument again.

06:16 So when you use the term Gāo Shān Liú Shuǐ, not only is it an exclamation of fine and beautiful music, comparing whatever you just heard to Yú Bóyá's Spring and Autumn classical pieces. It has a double meaning. Thanks to this story of Yu Boya and Zhong Ziqi taken from the Discourses of Lü Buwei, the Lüshi Chunqiu, this chengyu also describes true and pure friendship, or two soul mates, two friends whose bond was special and uncommon.

06:49 This piece of music is very well known to classical Chinese musicians and can be played on the gûzheng, pípa, qín and probably other instruments as well. You can go on YouTube if you have access to it in your country, and find there are many many videos of musicians playing Gāo Shān Liú Shuǐ. Hear it for yourself and see if you are moved by this as much as Zhōng Zǐqī was.

07:13 So that's our Chinese Saying for this time, another musical one at that. Yú Bóyá and Zhōng Zǐqī. Music was their bond and the spirit of their friendship was manifested in their mutual understanding and love of music.

23

CHINESE SAYINGS BOOK 2
EPISODE 4

07:27 | Until next time, this is your humble host and narrator Laszlo Montgomery coming to you as usual but not always, from the lovely little town of Los Angeles, located between San Diego and Santa Barbara. See you next time everyone.

Chinese Sayings Book 2
Episode 5

GIVE IT ALL YOU GOT!

一鼓作气—Yī Gǔ Zuò Qì

TRANSCRIPT

00:00 | Welcome everyone. Nice to see that you keep coming back to the well. Laszlo Montgomery here again with another nice musical chengyu for your ongoing edification.

00:13 | We're using a chengyu that comes from one of the greatest primary sources in ancient Chinese history. And as far as I know, we haven't drawn on this one yet for any Chinese Sayings, musical or otherwise. The work from which today's chengyu is derived is called the Zuǒ Zhuàn 左转. This work along with the Chūn Qiú 春秋 or Spring and Autumn Annals, written by Confucius, or so they say, are a couple of the most authoritative primary sources of the Spring & Autumn Period, that have made it to our time.

00:47 | So the Zuǒ Zhuàn is one hell of an important work that sheds some light on those Later Zhou Dynasty Days, more than twenty-five hundred years ago.

25

CHINESE SAYINGS BOOK 2
EPISODE 5

01:00	Let's look at the story behind Yī Gǔ Zuò Qì. But before we do though, let's plop this four syllable idiomatic phrase up on the slab and pick it apart character by character.
01:11	Yī Gǔ Zuò Qì.
01:14	Yī is the number one.
01:16	A Gǔ is a drum. Yī Gǔ, one drum.
01:22	Zuò means to make or to do and Qì, this means breath. If you're familiar with the subject of Qì Gōng, this is that character, Qì.
01:32	So line them all up in a row and we get One Drum Make Breath. Stop trying to figure it out. If you don't know the story from which this chengyu sprang, I'm telling you, you're wasting your time trying to guess.
01:47	So let's open up the Zuǒ Zhuàn and go to the chapter on the Ten Years of Duke Zhuāng, the sixteenth ruler of Lǔ State 鲁国, going all the way back to the oldest son of the Duke of Zhou himself. Co-starring in this production is Duke Zhuang of Lu's trusty military advisor Cáo Guì.
02:07	Lu State is somewhat of a sacred cow as far as all these Zhou Era kingdoms and states go. Confucius and Mòzǐ 墨子 both came from Lǔ. Shandong is referred to as Qí Lǔ Liángguó, the two kingdoms of Lu and Qi. Lu was in the south and Qí in the north. Combined, they pretty much made up the whole province of Shandong. Cars registered in Shandong province today have the

CHINESE SAYINGS BOOK 2
EPISODE 5

---

character Lu on their plates, harkening back to this fabled time in ancient Chinese history, the Zhou Dynasty.

02:43 We're in the year 684 BCE at the Battle of Chángsháo. The Kingdom of Qi was warring on the neighboring Kingdom of Lu to the south. And the two sides faced off outside of present day Láiwú. And as they did back in those days, the two opposing sides would face off on the battlefield and their respective battle drums would be beaten to summon the other side to combat.

03:11 All the sudden that familiar boom that stirred the blood of many ancient warriors was heard and felt. The numerically superior Qi army began pounding their battle drums to start the beginning of combat and to summon the Lu army to engage them. Duke Zhuang of Lu gave the order to his senior general to return the volley and sound the drums at once. However this senior general named Cáo Guì advised Duke Zhuang not to do this. He counseled his superior to hold off. Don't do anything yet. Wait for Qi to beat their drums again and then a third time before doing anything.

03:52 A second time and then shortly thereafter for a third time, the Qi army sounded their battle drums. Only after the third time did Cáo Guì tell Duke Zhuang of Lu that now was the time to advance and attack. So the sound of the Lu battle drums went out across the battlefield and with everyone's adrenaline flowing, forward the Lu army advanced. So hard and ferociously did these Lu soldiers fight that when it was all over, it was a resounding defeat for Qi. The Lu army totally overwhelmed them. And bravery was exhibited by his troops the likes that Duke Zhuang had never seen before.

04:35 That night after Lu soldiers were mopping up, Duke Zhuang asked Cáo Guì why he had stayed his hand when he had called for his drummers to return the Qi call for battle.

04:47 General Cáo Guì explained. In battle, at the very beginning when the drums are first beaten, a soldier's courage, morale and will to fight is at its highest. Then when it beats a second time, these feelings are diminished compared to the magnitude of a soldier's courage after hearing the first drum beats. By the third pounding of the drums, the courage of these soldiers will fall to the extent that their will to fight will be affected.

05:18 Then, explained Cáo Guì, we beat our drums for the first time and charged into battle when our soldiers' courage was at its peak. With one single pounding of the battle drums, we immediately rushed forward and overcame our less courageous enemy. When our will to fight, after the first beat of the drum, was at its peak, theirs on the Qi side was already greatly reduced. And therefore, although they outnumbered us greatly, we were able to defeat them.

05:47 Duke Zhuang of Lu nodded with understanding and said, I see what this means. With only one beating of our drums we gave all we got and in one sudden burst of energy, and with our will to fight at its peak, we

CHINESE SAYINGS BOOK 2
EPISODE 5

overcame Qi.

06:03 And so with Yī Gǔ, one beat of the drums, the army of Lu Zuò Qì expended all their energies and therefore, emerged victorious on that day back in 684 BCE.

06:16 Yī Gǔ Zuò Qì. That's a chengyu that you should keep tucked away for when you're in a situation where you're going to be required to give all you got in one single burst of energy. In trying to accomplish a difficult or perhaps seemingly impossible task, in one shot, you give all you got to achieve your objective.

06:34 Yī Gǔ Zuò Qì. I'm not sure I can come up with the English equivalent of this chengyu. In a single burst of energy, that's the best I can come up with.

06:45 So that's our Chinese Saying for this time. Let me see what musical Chinese Saying I can dig up for next time. I'm running out.

07:29 OK, until the next time this is your host, Laszlo Montgomery signing off on another perfect sunny day here in the capital of Southern California, Los Angeles. Thanks for popping by for a visit and a listen and I'll be hoping and praying you'll come back next time for another exciting episode of the Chinese Sayings Podcast.

Chinese Sayings Book 2 Episode 6

YOU SMELL THAT?

不知肉味—Bù Zhī Ròu Wèi

TRANSCRIPT

00:00 | Welcome back everyone. Last you're going to hearing from me and the Chinese Sayings Podcast for a while. This is the season finale. Time to disappear for a while like last time. Go take a little break. Maybe head to Mustique for a while to recharge. Laszlo Montgomery here with another musical chengyu, a Chinese Saying.

00:21 | I'll be honest with you I had to get a spatula and scrape the bottom of the pot here. I actually have about four remaining Chinese Sayings here that got slotted in the musical category. But after reading the stories, I have to be honest, nothing got me excited.

00:39 | But this one today stars Master Kong himself, Kongzi, better known in the English speaking world as Confucius. That's the one I decided to go with. And I can guarantee, unless you already know this story from the Lúnyû, the Analects of Confucius, you won't have a clue what these four characters mean.

CHINESE SAYINGS BOOK 2
EPISODE 6

01:00 | Now this one today has a four character and six character version. It's one of those. Either way, you're good. Let's tell the four-character version first and then in a minute I'll get to the deluxe version that offers the 50% premium on the amount of Chinese characters used in the idiom.

01:17 | Our chengyu for this week is Bù Zhī Ròu Wèi. Let's get right on it.

01:23 | Bù means no or not.

01:27 | Zhī means to know, the verb. Bùzhī, don't know.

01:32 | Ròu means meat, like beef, pork, and whatever.

01:35 | And wèi you may recall from back in season one Wèi Rú Jī Lèi, tastes like chicken ribs. Wei means the taste of something.

01:44 | So Bù Zhī Ròu Wèi. No know meat taste.

01:51 | Okay, something that has to do with not knowing the taste of meat. That much we can tell. But what does that mean?

01:57 | Well, I'll tell you. As I said, this story comes from the Analects, the Lunyu. One of the Four Books that were the main thing you had to memorize inside out if you had any aspirations whatsoever to serve in the imperial bureaucracy.

CHINESE SAYINGS BOOK 2
EPISODE 6

02:13 Because Confucius is in this story we know right away it takes place during the Chunqiu or Spring and Autumn Period, the first half of the second half of the Zhou Dynasty, to put it another way.

02:24 If you remember from a couple episodes ago Yigu Zuoqi, Confucius was from the State of Lu in Shandong. Their next-door neighbor to the north was the State of Qi. In the year 517 BCE, Confucius decided one day to go visit Qí and do a little studying at one of the local schools there.

02:46 As Confucius approached the outskirts of the Qí capital city of Línzī, he heard a musical sound coming from the forest where he was walking and he stopped and looked around and he saw an old man. The old guy was performing a kind of music not too many people listen to today, but this Sháo music supposedly went all the way back to Emperor Shun, one of the mythical Five Emperors. It was performed in this epic-style that combined poetry, music and dance and would lionize the good deeds of the mythical emperor Shun.

03:22 There are lots of references to this ancient Shao music that was played at the imperial court. But as I said, it all but died out and all that's left is what we read about it. None of the records or CDs survive.

03:35 And the reason we know this is because southwest of the ancient Qi, capital at Línzī, present day Zībó in Shandong, a stele was unearthed at a temple site during the Qing dynasty that claimed Confucius had visited once and listened to Shao music there.

CHINESE SAYINGS BOOK 2
EPISODE 6

03:55 | Well as the story goes, so enthusiastic an admirer of this ancient style of music did Confucius become, when he chanced upon this performer there, he couldn't stop listening. He kept going back to this place where the old man performed for three solid months to take it all in. So entranced and enamored was Confucius with this man performing Shao music, it's said he didn't even know the taste of meat, meaning so mesmerized was he by the music, the smell of roasting meat wafting around him went unnoticed.

04:30 | Bù zhī, he didn't know. Ròu wèi, the fragrance of the meat.

04:35 | And because he binged on Shao music for three months, we also have the deluxe version of this Chinese Saying: Sān Yuè. Sān means three and yuè means month. So Sān Yuè, three months. Bù Zhī Ròu Wèi, didn't know the taste of meat. In other words, if someone was grilling up a steak or lamb kebobs or something like that, no matter how pungent and tantalizing the smell was, it went completely unnoticed by the Great Sage because he was too enraptured by the sound of the Shao music.

05:09 | You know, not everyone could afford meat back then, so it sort of became a metaphor to describe something valuable that you don't get to enjoy regularly. Unless you were a strict vegetarian, having meat was special and not an everyday thing. So that's why it's particularly worth noting that even something like meat, Confucius didn't even notice.

CHINESE SAYINGS BOOK 2
EPISODE 6

05:32 | So when you're talking to someone about your friend or husband or whoever and that they had been utterly captivated by something to the extent that it appears as if they have lost touch with reality and can focus on nothing else, their Facebook page or some video game, you can say they Bù Zhī Ròu Wèi, couldn't even tell the smell of meat. Or if you want to add the optional two extra characters, Sān Yuè Bù Zhī Ròu Wèi. For three months he couldn't even notice the smell of meat.

06:02 | I'm not sure about the exact English equivalent. But that's what it means. So we'll just go with that. Bù Zhī Ròu Wèi, our chengyu that comes to us from the Spring and Autumn Period more than 2,500 years ago. A phrase lifted from the Analects of Confucius that's about as sacred a book as you can get as far as the philosophy of this Great Sage.

06:26 | And that is going to be that for now and for this season. Unless something terrible happens, I'll be back at a time of my choosing, to kick off season three. Not sure what the theme will be, but I'll make sure to find ten halfway decent chengyu to fill it up.

06:43 | Until that time, this is your host Laszlo Montgomery inviting you to go check out the other two fine shows here at Teacup Media, The China History Podcast and the China Vintage Hour. Take care everyone and I'll see you in a few weeks or so for another season of the Chinese Sayings Podcast.

**Chinese Sayings Book 2
Episode 7**

SEEING IS BELIEVING

百闻不如一见 — Bǎi Wén Bùrú Yī Jiàn

TRANSCRIPT

00:00 Hi everyone, I'm back again, Laszlo Montgomery with another nice Chinese Saying. This one is six characters long rather than the standard four. And if I may say in all humility, today's chengyu is perhaps the most useful one yet presented on this program. Well, top three maybe and top five for sure.

00:24 The old stalwart of many a book of chengyu: Bǎi Wén Bùrú Yī Jiàn.

00:30 Let's do the usual.

00:32 Bǎi means a hundred and wén means to hear. Bǎi Wén, to hear a hundred times.

00:40 The two characters, bùrú, mean not as good as or inferior to.

00:46 And yī means one, the number one.

CHINESE SAYINGS BOOK 2
EPISODE 7

00:49 | And jiàn means to see. Yījiàn, see one time.

00:53 | One hundred hear not as good as one see.

00:58 | This is one of those chengyu's where after you hear the characters strung together they make enough sense where the meaning is instantly revealed. This saying is the Chinese version of our English "seeing is believing" or a variation of "a picture's worth a thousand words." Well, the purpose of the Chinese Sayings Podcast isn't so much to introduce you to these idioms and sayings as much as it's about the ancient stories behind them.

01:22 | Bǎi Wén Bùrú Yī Jiàn... Let's check out the backstory.

01:26 | For this particular chengyu, we have to go back to the Western Han dynasty to the time of the emperor Xuān. He was one of the better Han emperors and got to sit on the throne for a nice long stint, from 74 to 49 BCE. Hàn Xuān Dì was the Chinese emperor whose reign was contemporary with the time of Pompey, Crassus, Cato, Julius Caesar and many of the other greats from Mike Duncan's History of Rome epic.

01:57 | Emperor Xuān was exploring ways to deal with this little problem he had in the west. The further west you went in China, the closer to Central Asia you came. And from the earliest times in Chinese history these people who rimmed the Middle Kingdom to the north and west, not Han Chinese, they gave China's rulers an endless supply of worry and headaches. The material wealth that all these nomadic tribes knew existed inside sedentary

CHINESE SAYINGS BOOK 2
EPISODE 7

China, was always a big draw for these invaders.

02:31   One of these people out west, near the Tibetan Plateau, where Sichuan and Tibet meet up, were a group called called the Qiāng. Today the Qiāng are one of the 56 official ethnic minority peoples recognized by the People's Republic of China government. There's maybe a couple hundred thousand or so around today.

02:50   But they weren't the exact same as the Qiāng people who lived out west during the Han Dynasty. The Qiāng, back then was sort of a catch-all term given to various groups of people who lived out that way and who were stressing out Han China with their incursions into Chinese territory. Today's Qiāng are perhaps partly descended from these people.

03:14   Emperor Xuān called his advisors together for a pow-wow to discuss solutions to this problem. One of the men present was named Zhào Chōngguó. He was a seventy-six year old grizzled veteran of many campaigns and had spent years, decades in fact, defending China's western territories and knew these Qiāng people better than most. He rose during the meeting to speak. And Zhào Chōngguó said that he, despite his advanced age, would be the most suitable one to go and deal with these invaders.

03:51   The emperor Xuān asked Zhào Chōngguó how he intended to deal with these people and how many troops he would require. General Zhao told the emperor it was impossible to devise a winning strategy without

CHINESE SAYINGS BOOK 2
EPISODE 7

first seeing for himself what the situation was out there. So according to the Qián Hàn Shū, The Book of Han, the official history written about this period up to Wang Mang's usurpation, Zhào Chōngguó took some of his men out west on a recon mission to go see for himself what was going on.

04:24 After careful observations and getting familiar with the lay of the land and the state of the Qiāng military and after capturing a few Qiāng soldiers and interrogating them as to the positions of the Qiāng armies, Zhào Chōngguó saw all that he had needed to see. At once he began to devise a strategy.

04:46 General Zhào knew what to do and after reporting back to his King, he organized a military expedition that indeed made fast work of the Qiāng and put an end to their incursions into Han Chinese territory.

04:58 In this official history of this time, the Book of Han, Zhào Chōngguó was immortalized not only as a great military man of the times but also as the one who gave us the chengyu, Bǎi Wén Bùrú Yī Jiàn.

05:12 Zhào Chōngguó said in order to figure out how to proceed he had to see for himself what was up. He insisted that Bǎi wén, to hear about something a hundred times, Bùrú, wasn't as good as, Yī Jiàn, seeing it one time. A picture's worth a thousand words. And this chengyu has been used millions and millions of times since and continues to be used into our very day here in the 21st century. And being the betting man that I am,

40

CHINESE SAYINGS BOOK 2
EPISODE 7

I'm sure in cultures around the world everyone has their own version of this one. Direct from the Qian Hàn Shū.

05:48　Bǎi Wén Bùrú Yī Jiàn, ladies and gentlemen. Zhao Chongguo's words to the Han Emperor Xuān regarding the Qiāng nation situated near the farthest upper reaches of the Yellow River.

05:59　Seeing is believing, a picture's worth a thousand words. Are there any more truer words than that?

06:05　I hope you liked that. This is one of the more useful Chinese sayings. Go try it out on your friends. And after they give you that quizzical look, you can personally school them as to its meaning. Then they can go spread the word.

06:19　So that's our chengyu for this time. Six syllables, fifty per cent more than usual, all at the same low price.

06:24　I hope you will consider possibly coming back next time for another offering. There's a lot more where that came from.

07:06　Until next time, me little beauties, this is your humble host and narrator Laszlo Montgomery, signing off as usual from sunny and beautiful Los Angeles. City in the Smog. Don't you wish that you could be here too? See you next time. Bye all!

**Chinese Sayings Book 2
Episode 8**

THERE'S ALWAYS A WAY

有志者事竟成 (有志竟成)—Yǒu zhì zhě shì jìng chéng

TRANSCRIPT

00:00 | Hello again everyone, Laszlo Montgomery here for the seventh time this heroic season 3, bringing you yet another flavorful and utterly satisfying Chinese Saying, another chengyu for your growing collection.

00:16 | Last episode, we traveled to the Western or Former Han Dynasty. This time we're at the commencement of the Eastern or Later Han. The dynasty is back in business after the fall of the Western Han and a brief interregnum with Wáng Mǎng. If you caught China History Podcast episodes 19 and 20, you know what I'm talking about. For now, at least in this episode, there's a good emperor on the throne in Luòyáng. And this good emperor is one of our stars today in this Chinese Saying.

00:49 | His surname was Liú, like all the emperors of the Han Dynasty. Liú Xiù was his name and he's best known to followers of Chinese history as the Emperor Hàn Guāngwǔ. He was the first emperor of the Eastern Han Dynasty that lasted a hundred ninety-five years.

CHINESE SAYINGS BOOK 2
EPISODE 8

01:07 | Our chengyu today has an asterisk next to it. One of those again. There's the four character version that I'm going to show you. And then there's also a version that contains a total of six characters, like last episode. We'll look at both of these versions. But I want to assure you if you only can remember the four-character variant, that'll work in every case.

01:29 | Yǒu means to have.

01:31 | Zhì means will or determination. Yǒu zhì, to have the will or determination

01:38 | Jìng means to finish or complete something.

01:42 | And chéng in this case means to accomplish or succeed. Jìng chéng means to finish and accomplish.

01:50 | And we quickly look at the longer six-character version: Yǒu zhìzhě shì jìng chéng. Yǒu zhìzhě goes from to have the will to the person who has the will. Adding that zhě particle to the end of zhì changes the meaning from the will to the one who has will.

02:08 | Shì jìng chéng. Shì means matters or affairs, things to do, business. And again, jìng means to finish or complete and chéng, to accomplish. Jìng chéng, finish and accomplish.

02:22 | So you lay it all out and you get: Someone of will, matters, finish accomplish. Sounds awkward when you put it like that but string it all together in Chinese Yǒu zhìzhě shì jìng chéng or the simpler four-character version: Yǒu zhì

44

CHINESE SAYINGS BOOK 2
EPISODE 8

jìng chéng, that's the Chinese equivalent to our English "where there's a will there's a way".

02:45   This saying just didn't appear out of nowhere. Someone famous said it first and it got written down in one of the official histories that survived to our day. The Hòu Hàn Shū 后汉书 to be exact. The book of the Later Han, compiled in the 5th century. Last episode we looked at the Qian Han Shū 前汉书, the Book of Former Han. This is the Book of Later Han.

03:06   It mentions in one of the chapters at the start of the Eastern Han, there was a scholar named Gěng Yǎn. At an early age he was wowed by the mounted soldiers he once saw pass through his village, swinging their swords and looking all soldierly-like. Even though he wasn't born into that world, this is what he aspired to. His father was a military figure around the Zhangjiakou-Beijing area. Using his father's connections made it easier for Gěng Yǎn to make the transition from aspiring scholar to soldier.

03:43   So when Gěng Yǎn heard or read that Liú Xiù, the future Guāngwǔ emperor, was recruiting men to fight in his army, he saw his chance and he took it. And in the course of several years after joining up, Gěng Yǎn made a name for himself. He won many victories and had received accolades from Liú Xiù.

04:01   So the year 28 CE rolls around and Liú Xiù is now the Emperor Guāngwǔ. And he has a major headache on his hands. He fought his way to the emperorship and after

CHINESE SAYINGS BOOK 2
EPISODE 8

that long interregnum with Wáng Mǎng, he put the Liu clan back on the Han imperial throne. But there was still a whole bunch of mopping up to do. Chiang Kai-shek would have this same problem nineteen centuries later. All over the north of China there were these warlords who had set themselves up and had dug in deep during the period in between the Western and Eastern Han. If the Guāngwǔ Emperor was going to unify the whole of China, these guys had to be dealt with.

04:42 The emperor called on his best guys and said they had to go out and handle this. Quell all these warlords and bring those lands back under direct Han imperial control. Gěng Yǎn was ordered to deal with one of these named Zhāng Bù who was based in and around Shandong. It was no secret that Zhāng Bù's warlord army was one of the bigger and more powerful ones. Gěng Yǎn nonetheless devised a plan to take him down.

05:10 Zhāng Bù's army had the numerical superiority, but Gěng Yǎn attacked him in three places, surprising his army and bloodying their noses. Zhāng Bù, so sure of himself due to his numerical superiority, didn't think much of Gěng Yǎn. Although he got hit hard, Zhāng Bù with his 20,000 troops, felt certain he could get rid of this guy.

05:32 The showdown between Zhāng Bù and Gěng Yǎn happened in Línzī, the ancient capital of the Qí State, located in present-day Zībó, Shāndōng Province. Just to the east of the city, the two armies clashed. In the first encounter, with the warlord Zhāng Bù personally

CHINESE SAYINGS BOOK 2
EPISODE 8

leading his troops into battle, Gěng Yǎn got hit by a flying arrow that went straight into his thigh. Ouch! The fighting was fierce. It was a lot more up close and personal back in those days. Try as he might, Zhāng Bù's army with its numerical superiority still couldn't overwhelm Gěng Yǎn's forces.

06:10 Someone had sent word back to the palace in Luòyáng that Gěng Yǎn's army was pinned down and on the verge of defeat. The Guāngwǔ Emperor, upon hearing this news called at once for an army to head east to aid Gěng Yǎn. And the Emperor said he would lead this army himself.

06:27 Meanwhile back in Línzī Gěng Yǎn's army was back on its heels. His officers, in their despair, said Zhāng Bù's forces couldn't be beat. The best course of action was to pull back, regroup and wait for the reinforcements that were on the way. Luoyang was about a ten-day march from Línzī.

06:46 Gěng Yǎn stood before his men and ordered them to prepare a sacrifice and a feast to welcome the Emperor. He asked his men how could they possibly welcome His Majesty without first completing their mission? If the emperor arrived and Zhāng Bù was still a threat to them, all it would do is make the Emperor worry. Therefore he ordered everyone to gear up, lock and load and they were going to go out and deal with Zhāng Bù decisively. In this way, when the Guāngwǔ emperor arrived at their camp, they could receive him victorious and tell him he had one less headache to deal with.

47

CHINESE SAYINGS BOOK 2
EPISODE 8

07:25 | Gěng Yǎn led with determination, stamina, and exhibited before his troops this sheer will to win. It served as a model for his men who before long rose to the occasion, beat back Zhāng Bù and soundly defeated his army, sending the warlord's surviving troops fleeing for their lives.

07:46 | By the time the Guāngwǔ emperor arrived in Línzī, Gěng Yǎn was just finishing up and you can't imagine what a celebration they had. The emperor regaled Gěng Yǎn, comparing him to the general Hán Xìn of the Western Han whose victories on the battlefield gave Emperor Wǔ, Hàn Wǔdì, the solid foundation upon which to grow the country. Guāngwǔ told Gěng Yǎn he had done the same as Hán Xìn and now the Han dynasty was more secure.

08:18 | And it was here where the Guāngwǔ Emperor, in praising Gěng Yǎn said the magic words, If someone has the will, Yǒu Zhìzhe, they'll find a way, Shìjìngchéng. Where there's a will, there's a way. And this was later shortened to Yǒu Zhì jìng chéng. And these four characters, these four syllables, describe someone who will brave every disaster and setback, fight against the odds, overcome any obstacle to achieve what they set out to accomplish.

08:50 | Yǒu Zhì, if you have the will. Jìng chéng, completion will result in success. Thank you, Emperor Han Guāngwǔ.

08:58 | Well, there it is. This is Laszlo Montgomery signing off from lovely and scenic Los Angeles California. I'll see you again soon, I hope I'm guessing in another seven days, for another heroic episode of the Chinese Sayings Podcast.

Chinese Sayings Book 2 Episode 9

ALWAYS EXPECT THE UNEXPECTED

万事俱备, 只欠东风—Wàn Shì Jùbèi Zhǐ Qiàn Dōngfēng

TRANSCRIPT

00:00 Greetings everyone all across the universe, Laszlo Montgomery here. The Season 3 finale for you. That was the fastest ten weeks I ever experienced. Wán Bì Guī Zhào 完璧归赵 seems like only yesterday. You're really gonna get your money's worth today. For the same low-low price you've been paying for all these past CSP episodes, you're getting a two-fer this time. Today's chengyu is eight characters long. Yikes! But it's another useful one and has quite an excellent pedigree.

00:33 So let's not waste any more time with all this idle chit-chat and polite talking. Let's break this long Chinese Saying down into its constituent parts. Wànshì Jùbèi, Zhǐ Qiàn Dōngfēng.

00:49 Okay, first four.

00:51 Wàn means ten thousand and shì means matter, affair or a thing to do. So, wànshì, ten thousand things to do, or ten thousand matters. That's how you say the word

CHINESE SAYINGS BOOK 2
EPISODE 9

	everything in Chinese. Wànshì, ten thousand things.
01:12	Jù means all or complete and bèi means to prepare. Jùbèi, all prepared.
01:19	Wànshì Jùbèi, everything's all prepared.
01:24	Now the second set of four characters, Zhǐ Qiàn Dōngfēng.
01:28	Zhǐ means only. And qiàn means to lack or to owe. Zhǐ qiàn, only lack.
01:40	And dōng means east and fēng is wind. Dōngfēng, the east wind.
01:48	Zhǐ Qiàn Dōngfēng. Only lack the east wind.
01:54	And after we string together all eight characters: it ends up sounding like this: everything all prepared, Only lack the east wind. Sounds heroic already. I can't wait to hear the story behind it.
02:08	Lovers of Luó Guànzhōng's epic work Romance of the Three Kingdoms no doubt have already figured this one out. Romance of the Three Kingdoms, the classic novel, was a fictionalized account of the main events from China's Three Kingdoms period, 220 to 280. This period was the cushion between the end of the Eastern Han Dynasty and the beginning of the Western Jin. Most of the people in Luó Guànzhōng's novel were actual historic people. But a lot of the stories, like the one I'm

CHINESE SAYINGS BOOK 2
EPISODE 9

about to tell you, are fiction based on fact. This novel yielded some nice chéngyǔ's, including this one.

02:51 The background event for this story is the Battle of Red Cliffs or Chìbì 赤壁. That incredible naval battle happened right on the Yangzi River not far from Wuhan, a city in China that has witnessed more than its fair share of historic events in both ancient and modern times.

03:10 Our story happened at the tail end of the year 208 and the start of the year 209. The Eastern Hàn Dynasty at this time, 208-209, was still in existence, though not for long. The Hàn emperor Xiàn was kept in the pocket of the mighty chancellor Cáo Cāo and was merely a puppet at this stage. Cáo Cāo's power base was in the north of China where the emperor resided. He had this idea to one day set himself up as emperor of his own dynasty.

03:44 Opposing Cáo Cāo was a shaky alliance between the two power bases in the south of China. Liú Bèi, from last episode, those flabby thighs, based in the west and Sūn Quán in the east. These two enemies of Cáo Cāo had agreed to join forces to overcome the much more powerful armies to the north.

04:07 It was now four centuries after Liú Bāng founded the Han Dynasty in 206 BCE. The power of his once great ruling house had dissolved into these three contending kingdoms all keen to seize the Mandate of Heaven.

04:24 So this Battle of Chìbì was meant to be a kind of knock-out punch from Cáo Cāo to both Liú Bèi and Sūn Quán.

CHINESE SAYINGS BOOK 2
EPISODE 9

He advanced south with overwhelming force and with a massive navy.

04:38 I said this alliance between Liú Bèi and Sūn Quán was shaky. Two of their main men on each side, Zhūgé Liàng representing Shǔ Hàn and Zhōu Yú representing Sūn Wú. They both had to work together to come up with a plan to defeat Cáo Cāo. But neither trusted the other. And as the big showdown at Chìbì was getting closer, Zhōu Yú came up with a brainstorm to use one of his trusted generals Huáng Gài to feign defection, and lead a whole small flotilla of ships in Cao Cao's direction.

05:18 Those on the south side of the Yángzǐ saw how Cáo Cāo's navy of landlubber northerners was all roped together in a line to keep the vessels steady and in a tight formation. No Dramamine back in those days. So those troops were as seasick as could be. The Yángzǐ River wasn't some quiet stream or bubbling brook.

05:41 Zhōu Yú's secret plan called for Huáng Gài's ships to sail with the winds that reliably blew from the southeast at this time of year. The winds would blow the ships across the river from southeast to the northwest. And as soon as they got within striking distance, Huáng Gài's men would torch their ships that were filled with all kinds of incendiary materials. They'd jump overboard and the East winds would just blow these fire ships right into Cao Cao's unwitting navy, all tightly tied together, and the whole armada in one fell swoop would get flamed.

CHINESE SAYINGS BOOK 2
EPISODE 9

06:19 | When the moment came, Zhōu Yú had everything in place. But wouldn't you know it, his best laid plans, so meticulously put together down to the smallest detail, ended up being all for nothing. Wànshì Jùbèi, everything was prepared except for one thing, zhǐ qiàn Dōng fēng. He only lacked the east winds. On that day, at that crucial hour, the winds were still.

06:46 | So Zhōu Yú was rather dejected and his rival Zhūgé Liàng stepped in. First he wrote a poem to Zhōu Yú and it was in this poem that he wrote those immortal words, Wànshì Jùbèi, zhǐ qiàn Dōng fēng. You had everything prepared except for the East Winds.

07:07 | So for the next three days, Zhūgé Liàng carried out all these rituals and ceremonies. And then whatever he did to appease the spirits worked because when they gave it another go a few days later, the winds started blowing briskly and reliably from the east and this time Zhōu Yú's plan to use fire ships found their mark and Cáo Cāo's navy got partially incinerated and he suffered a devastating defeat.

07:36 | That wasn't the decisive battle between the Three Kingdoms. Just one of them. But a big one. And I said after this Chìbì zhīzhàn or Battle of Red Cliffs, there's still more than a decade to go before Cáo Cāo dies along with the Han Dynasty. That will mark the official start of the Three Kingdoms period that begins in 220. Cáo Cāo's son will go on to found that Cáo Wèi dynasty that had eluded him.

CHINESE SAYINGS BOOK 2
EPISODE 9

08:07 | Let me tell you, John Woo directed a four-hour epic film on this Battle of Red Cliff. So my little one minute encapsulation barely does this milestone in Chinese history justice. Let me recommend the movie Chìbì, Red Cliffs if you never saw it. Directed by John Woo.

08:54 | So Wàn shì jùbèi, everything was totally prepared. But the plan failed because zhǐ qiàn dōng fēng, it only lacked the east wind. And without the east wind it didn't matter how well prepared Zhōu Yú was.

09:11 | This is a situation I'm sure all of us have run up against one time or another. You set out to do something and the one thing you didn't think of, after you planned everything down to the smallest detail, didn't happen. And your whole big idea went down the old proverbial toilet.

09:28 | A nice picnic at the park? You went out the day before and bought everything, packed it all up the night before. But when you woke up the next morning it was pouring rain.

09:39 | Wànshì Jùbèi Zhi Qiàn Dōngfēng. I hope you don't have to use this one anytime soon.

09:45 | Okay, that's it for our heroic episode this week. Laszlo Montgomery here signing off from LA for the final time this Season 3. That was a fast ten weeks if you ask me. Please don't throw in the towel just yet. I'm going to go recharge my batteries and think up ten more nice chengyu's for you in Season Four. I'll see you when I see you. Take care everyone.

Chinese Sayings Book 2
Episode 10

WAITING IN VAIN

守株待兔—Shǒu Zhū Dài Tù

TRANSCRIPT

00:00	Welcome back everyone. Thanks for returning. Laszlo Montgomery here with another Chinese Saying.
00:09	Today's chéngyǔ is gonna be brief. I always liked this one. A textbook chéngyǔ. Shǒu Zhū Dài Tù.
00:16	Let's do the usual. See what these individual characters mean. Only four as usual.
00:23	Shǒu means to guard something or keep watch.
00:26	The second character Zhū means a tree trunk or tree stump.
00:31	Dài means to wait for. And a rabbit is called a tù.
00:35	Guard tree stump wait rabbit.
00:40	This is one of those that might leave you stumped. If you knew not the tale behind Shǒu Zhū Dài Tù. So let's tell

CHINESE SAYINGS BOOK 2
EPISODE 10

the story. As I said, it's a quickie.

00:50 This story first appeared in that great classic of Legalist philosophy from the Warring States period, the Hán Fēizǐ. And if you turn to the chapter entitled Wǔ Dù 韩非子 — 五蠹, The Five Vermin, you'll find this one.

01:06 And it goes like this. There was this farmer who tended a small field in his home state of Sòng. If you caught the CHP episode on Henan History you'll recall Sòng was located in present day eastern Henan, western Shandong, with its capital where Shāngqiū is today.

01:23 This farmer was out in his fields one day doing all the hard work that farming entails. And after a while he decided to sit down and take a break. He leaned back against this old tree stump and relaxed.

01:38 Then out of nowhere he sees this rabbit sprinting at full speed, probably fleeing from some predator and wouldn't you know it, he runs into the tree stump full speed and is killed instantly from the impact.

01:51 And the farmer, wide-eyed and incredulous at what he just saw, couldn't believe his good fortune. Did this really happen?

02:01 He brought that rabbit back to his home and made a terrific stew that night. And as he enjoyed this most excellent dinner, he got to thinking. If this happened once, surely it'll happen again. And he began to get these notions that, why in the heck should he continue

CHINESE SAYINGS BOOK 2
EPISODE 10

the life of subsistence farming? As long as he gets his rabbit per day, that's all he needed. And no need to work so hard in the fields!

02:26 So the next day he got up and went straight to that tree stump and sat himself down and waited. His fellow villagers saw him sitting there and wondered what the hell was he doing, not working his fields?

02:40 But the farmer didn't mind them, and he sat where he was remaining fully alert for the moment another rabbit ran into this tree stump and thereby providing him with another delectable meal.

02:51 But after a few days, not one rabbit. Not even any close calls. But he refused to give up and felt certain if he just was little more patient another rabbit would come along and crash into that tree stump just like the one the previous week.

03:08 He waited long enough whereby his fields began to look pretty barren. And without the hard work required to maintain them, his crops started to fail and before long it became a wasteland. And word began to spread far and wide throughout the State of Sòng about this foolish farmer who guarded a tree stump waiting for a rabbit to crash into it.

03:31 He shǒu zhū, guarded that tree stump. And then he dài tù, waited for that rabbit. He waited for fortune to smile upon him like it had done once before and deliver another rabbit for his cooking pot. Like some people who sit around and wait for good luck to just fall into their lap, money, a new job, a new love in their life. Maybe you received some sign or something happened whereby you feel, hey I'm due for a little change in my fortunes. I was lucky once before and, believing if it happened once before, you feel certain it'll happen again.

04:07   And the lesson taught here is that just because you believe you're due and because you may have encountered some good luck previously, you felt, why do I have to work so hard or leave my comfort zone to achieve what I want? You convince yourself it happened before, it'll happen again. And only after too much time slips away do you realize your folly of waiting to get what you want rather than working hard to get it.

04:34   The context that Hán Fēizǐ used for this chéngyǔ in the chapter of his eponymous book was with regard to one of the great issues of his day. What constituted a good ruler. You see, in his time, the Warring States period of the Eastern Zhou Dynasty, this was one of the main arguments. What traits made the best rulers for the people? Guys like Confucius and Mèngzǐ and these other philosophers of the Rú School claimed that men of high virtue and righteousness were the most ideal candidates. And that those who emulated the great sage kings of yore, like Yáo, Shùn and Yǔ the Great, would make the best ruler of the people.

05:21   But Hán Fēi, he thought this was all nonsense and these kinds of men, virtuous they may be, by using these ancient kings as their guide, would be useless in these

CHINESE SAYINGS BOOK 2
EPISODE 10

Warring States days that were way more sophisticated than those centuries past. Different times required a different kind of ruler, which was what Legalism was all about.

05:43 Hán Fēi used this example of the farmer and the rabbit to explain his point that waiting around for some virtuous man like Yáo to come around and save the day was no different than this farmer in Sòng State waiting for that second rabbit to come crashing into that tree stump he was leaning against day after day.

06:04 So if you find yourself acting like this farmer, believing fortune will smile on you because it happened once before, and you give up trying and working hard to achieve what you set out to accomplish, you are just plain old Shǒu Zhū Dài Tù. You're guarding a tree stump and waiting for a rabbit.

06:22 That's not to say lightning won't strike twice. But it's better to be proactive sometimes rather than to passively wait for something to happen.

06:31 Shǒu Zhū Dài Tù. Don't do it. So, that's that. I told you this one wouldn't run too long. Trust me when I say there's a lot more where this came from. Do consider coming back for more.

06:44 This is Laszlo Montgomery signing off from LA California. Imploring you to considering coming back again next time for another good and decent chengyu here at the Chinese Sayings Podcast.

Chinese Sayings Book 2
Episode 11

SHOWING PAUL HOW TO WRITE A SONG

班门弄斧—Bān Mén Nòng Fǔ

TRANSCRIPT

00:00 | Welcome back everyone. Thanks for returning. Laszlo Montgomery here with another Chinese Saying.

00:08 | Today we examine an old idiom that's been popular for centuries and really serves as a great metaphor for certain situations. Let's look at this story and see why.

00:18 | Bān Mén Nòng Fǔ. Even going character by character, this one has no apparent meaning.

00:25 | Bān in this example is just the given name of a person who this story is all about.

00:30 | Mén is a door or gate.

00:34 | Nòng is a character that means to play with or fool with or to do something.

00:39 | And a Fǔ is an axe or a hatchet.

CHINESE SAYINGS BOOK 2
EPISODE 11

00:42 | Bān's door play with an axe.

00:46 | Let's not waste any time trying to figure out what this means. Unless you're familiar with this story, it's damn near impossible to crack the code for the hidden meaning behind these four characters.

00:57 | This one concerns a man who lived during the Eastern Zhou Dynasty, either during the Spring and Autumn or Warring States Period, not sure. But we're talking more than two thousand years ago. And this gent's name was said to be Gōngshū Bān 公输般 and he was born in the same Warring State who gave us Confucius, the state of Lǔ in southwest Shandong.

01:08 | Gōngshū was one of those 2-character compound surnames. I never met any Gōngshū's in my life. Besides Ōuyáng, Sīmǎ, and Sītú, this one, Gōngshū… not too common.

01:31 | After he moved to the State of Chǔ, centered around present day Húběi, Gōngshū Bān became known as Lǔ Bān. It was a different character Bān from what he was born with but it was pronounced exactly the same. And they called him by the surname Lǔ because that's where he came from, Lǔ State.

01:51 | During his time in Chǔ, living in the capital at Yǐng 郢, right on the Yángzǐ River near present day Jīngzhōu 荆州, he worked as a woodworker. Back in his time, Chǔ was constantly at war with its neighbors, mostly the state of Yuè located in present-day Zhèjiāng Province.

CHINESE SAYINGS BOOK 2
EPISODE 11

02:10 Yuè was always defeating Chǔ in battle and Lǔ Bān was determined to reverse this trend by putting his skills to work for the government creating all kinds of weapons of war that proved very effective in battle, both on land and on water. And he became respected throughout Chǔ for not only these machines and weapons he invented but also for the bridges and government buildings be designed and built.

02:36 Other woodworkers and craftsmen who were familiar with Lǔ Bān's work called him the zǔshī 祖师 or founder of his craft. This was an honorary title given to certain people who were respected for their virtuosity in their professions or for religious sects they led. He was truly revered in his day for his handiwork and for how much it had done for the land he called home, the state of Chǔ.

03:03 And in the centuries that followed his passing, Lǔ Bān was celebrated by others for his craftsmanship and the value he created for the state. The first one to give a nod to Lǔ Bān was the Táng Dynasty poet Liǔ Zōngyuán 柳宗元, who mentioned Lǔ Bān in his Preface to the Singing and Poems of Wáng Bózhòng 王伯仲. Oūyáng Xiū as well, he alluded to Lǔ Bān in one of his writings. Both literary masters, Liǔ Zōngyuán in the Táng and Oūyáng Xiū in the Sòng acknowledged Lǔ Bān's greatness at his craft and the ridiculousness of mediocrities who tried to compare themselves to him.

03:45 Perhaps the best known one involved a late Míng Dynasty scholar who's name was Méi Zhīhuàn 梅之焕 who one day went down to Ānhuī province to the town

CHINESE SAYINGS BOOK 2
EPISODE 11

off Dāngtú, not very far from the major city of Mǎ'ānshān where the tomb of Lǐ Bái 李白 was located. It's still there today, if you want to go pay your respects to one of the greatest poets in Chinese history.

04:08 When Méi Zhīhuàn stood before Lǐ Bái's tomb, there were many others there as well. And these people paying their respects to Lǐ Bái wrote poems and pasted them on a wall in front of the tomb which, like a lot of graves in China, was a small mound, like a mini hill.

04:27 It's said that at this location in Dāngtú one night, Lǐ Bái, who was known almost as much for his love of wine as his mastery of poetry, stood on the riverbank and stared at his reflection in the moonlight. And in his drunken attempt to embrace his image reflected in the water, fell into the river and drowned.

04:47 So Méi Zhīhuàn, upon seeing all these would-be poets leaving behind their poems at the tomb of this master was inspired to write the words: Cǎi shí jiāng biān yī duī tǔ, Lǐ Bái zhī míng gāo qiāngǔ; lái lái wǎngwǎng yī shǒu shī, Lǔ Bān ménqián nòng dà fǔ. 采石江边一堆土，李白之名高千古；来来往往一首诗，鲁班门前弄大斧.

05:13 And that translated to: along the banks of this river, there is a mound of earth (meaning Lǐ Bái's grave). Lǐ Bái's name is eternal; people come and leave behind poems, but are like those handling an axe before Lǔ Bān's door.

05:31 So he was comparing these mediocrities leaving behind poems at the great poet's tomb to someone showing off

CHINESE SAYINGS BOOK 2
EPISODE 11

their skills with an axe before the front door of Lǔ Bān's home. This is used to describe someone bragging about their particular skills in front of a true master of the art.

05:49 There's another saying similar to this one that goes Guān Gōng miànqián shuǎ dàdāo 关公面前耍大刀. To swing one's sword around in front of Guān Gōng, a hero from the Three Kingdoms who was known for his skills swinging his giant sword, the so-called Green Dragon Crescent Blade. Once again, meant to describe someone showing off their swordsmanship in front of one of the greatest to ever wield a sword.

06:16 So when you see someone bragging about how great they are at a certain skill in front of a real master, they are Bān Mén Nòng Fǔ. Bān Mén, in front of Lǔ Bān's door, they Nòng Fǔ, show off their skills with an axe. A novice showing off in front of an expert.

06:35 And just like the chéngyǔ introduced in Season 2, Làn Yú Chōng Shù 滥竽充数, to describe someone of no talent, you can also use Bān Mén Nòng Fǔ in a self-deprecating way when you are masterful at something and others around you sing your praises. With a wave of your hand you can say you are only Bān Mén Nòng Fǔ, a novice performing in front of a master. You modestly proclaim that you dare not perform in front of real experts.

07:03 If you're presenting your work to others for comment you can also say Bān Mén Nòng Fǔ. I'm just like someone showing off in front of real experts. So you can use this one to deride someone showing off in front of their betters or to show modesty in downplaying your mastery of something.

07:20 So keep that one handy for one day when you want to put someone in their place for bragging or showing off in front of anyone that's better than them at what their bragging about. And for acting modestly, downplaying your particular skill.

07:40 And let's just leave it at that. Laszlo Montgomery once again signing off from LA California, recommending you find ten minutes in your busy schedule to join me next time for another useful chengyu here at The Chinese Sayings Podcast.

 Chinese Sayings Book 2
Episode 12

NOBODY LOVES YOU WHEN YOU'RE DOWN AND OUT

门可罗雀—Mén Kě Luó Què

TRANSCRIPT

00:00 | Welcome back again ladies and gentlemans to another useful and interesting Chéngyǔ or Chinese Saying. Laszlo Montgomery here to present one that came straight out of the Records of the Grand Historian, the Shǐ Jì, Sīmǎ Qiān's magnum opus and the source of so much history from the Han Dynasty and before.

00:21 | Today's entry concerns something I'm sure every one of us is familiar with. Mén Kě Luó Què. Let's see if we can guess the meaning from the four characters.

00:33 | Mén Kě Luó Què.

00:36 | A mén is a door or gate.

00:39 | And Kě means to approve, be willing to, or can, as in you can do this.

00:46 | And Luó, aside from being a common surname means a net for catching birds, a sieve or silk gauze.

CHINESE SAYINGS BOOK 2
EPISODE 12

00:54 | And a què is a sparrow.

00:57 | And together the literal meaning is Door able to catch sparrows.

01:04 | Doesn't mean much on its own, but after I tell you this quick story about a Lord Zhái of Xiàguī 下邽 you'll be in on the secret. Xiàguī is a town located forty-five minutes north of the city of Wèinán 渭南 and maybe an hour and a half from the capital of Shǎnxī province, Xīān. He lived during the time of Han Emperor Wǔ, during the 2nd century BCE.

01:30 | He served his country ably as the Tíng Wèi 廷尉 which was the highest judicial office in the land. And Zhái Gōng, Duke Zhái, he was as capable a minister as they came and respected and admired by all who knew of him.

01:47 | And like it was back then as well eight thousand kilometers away in Rome, someone as noble as Duke Zhái had a lot of clients and hangers-on who hung out with him and gathered at his residence and filled his courtyard to show their respect or air their grievances or thoughts. And so great were the numbers of people who came to his door on a daily basis, those just passing by had to walk around the immense crowd of well-wishers and clients.

02:17 | Whoever could get close to Duke Zhái would bend over backwards to be of assistance to him and curry favor and show him their deepest respect and admiration.

CHINESE SAYINGS BOOK 2
EPISODE 12

02:28   And it was like this all the time. He was so popular and beloved of all the local people near that part of Shǎnxī near the Hàn capital at Cháng'ān.

02:36   And those who got face time with Zhái Gōng would bow and scrape before him and declare their everlasting loyalty and respect to him, declaring they would be loyal to him for all their days and their faith in him would never fade. Some even went so far as to tell the Duke he was more dear to them than their own mothers and fathers and swore they would be as loyal to him as dogs and horses are to their masters.

03:06   Then one day, and this was so common back in those days, and pretty much all the way through to the end of the Qīng Dynasty, someone or some people whispered to the emperor behind his back making all kinds of false claims about Duke Zhái's integrity, job performance and disloyalty, even saying he was an unfair judge.

03:28   Emperor Wǔ was swayed enough whereby he stripped Duke Zhái of all his rank and privileges and made him nothing more than a mere commoner. Boy, what could be worse than that? And practically overnight the crowds of hundreds of people who daily came to his residence and clamored for a few minutes of his time, disappeared. No one came anymore. And in fact, they all went on to find a new powerful and influential official who they could ally themselves to.

03:58   After such a sudden and dramatic fall, Duke Zhái was left with no one who wished to call him a friend or who

CHINESE SAYINGS BOOK 2
EPISODE 12

would give him any face. And his courtyard where people once stood shoulder to shoulder was empty and eerily quiet. And so quiet in fact, replacing all the people were hundreds of birds instead. And they made themselves at home outside the door of Duke Zhái's residence.

04:25 In fact so many were all these birds, if you simply hung a net in the courtyard you could snare a flock of them. So you can start to see where this chéngyǔ, Mén Kě Luó Què, is sort of heading.

04:38 Well, let me cut to the chase and just say that one day, Emperor Wǔ of Hàn learned that he had misjudged Zhái Gōng and not only did he restore him to his position of Tíng Wèi but like the good Lord did to Job in the Bible, he even rewarded him to the extent that he had more wealth than ever before his fall.

05:00 And wouldn't you know it, all those people who had abandoned him when he was out of favor... they all returned. And they hung out in his courtyard, outside his door. And as if nothing ever happened they went back to the way they had been before he had suffered his temporary political downfall. They had no shame.

05:21 And Zhái Gōng, he was privately disgusted at all this and learned a hard lesson. So for all to see, he took his ink brush and wrote twenty-four large Chinese characters in verse that said, "一生一死，乃知交情。一贫一富，乃知交态。一贵一贱，交情乃见 — Yīshēng yīsǐ, nǎi zhījiāoqīng. Yī pín yī fù, nǎi zhī jiāo tài. Yī guì

CHINESE SAYINGS BOOK 2
EPISODE 12

yī jiàn, jiāoqíng nǎi xiàn. Which translated to "Through life and death, one may know the true meanings of one's friends. Through wealth and poverty, one may know the true characters of one's friends. Through gaining and then losing my noble title, I have been shown the true intentions of my friends."

06:11 And upon seeing this calligraphy displayed in his courtyard, these fair-weather friends got the hint and slowly departed one by one, ashamed for being called out by Duke Zhái for revealing their true character. Talk is cheap. And just saying they were loyal meant nothing. As soon as Lord Zhǎi lost his position of power and authority, his friends abandoned him. And as soon as his good name was restored, everybody was trying to be his baby now. And they all clamored to be his friend tell him how much he meant to them.

06:47 So this one, Mén Kě Luó Què, at the 门 or door of Duke Zhái's home, you could ensnare sparrows, Kě Luó Què, because there were so many and no mobs of people to get in the way.

07:01 Save this one for all your BFFs who don't have time for you, or any fair-weather friend circling your orbit. Mén Kě Luó Què. Or if you run a business and your customers swore they'd never leave you but your place is empty, Mén Kě Luó Què.

07:19 Don't forget the immortal words of the 1923 blues standard by Jimmie Cox made famous in our day by Mr. Eric Clapton, "Nobody knows you when you're down

CHINESE SAYINGS BOOK 2
EPISODE 12

and out." Ain't it the truth! You got that right, Cowardly Lion.

07:35 Okay, that's gonna be it. A quick one this time, but nonetheless a chéngyǔ with a deep and profound meaning. Stick by your friends, especially if they've stood by you.

07:47 Okay, that's your Chinese Saying for this time. This is Laszlo Montgomery signing off from Los Angeles California imploring you to come back next time for another educational and informative episode of the Chinese Sayings Podcast.

Chinese Sayings Book 2
Episode 13

KNOCK KNOCK KNOCKIN' ON HEAVEN'S DOOR

釜底游魚—Fǔ Dǐ Yóu Yú

TRANSCRIPT

00:00 | Greetings once again everyone, Laszlo Montgomery here with the season four finale, a good one for you from the Eastern Hàn Dynasty featuring a scoundrel we mentioned back in a CHP episode number 267 if my memory serves me well. That was Part 1 of that six-part series on the Eunuchs in Chinese history.

00:24 | Today's chéngyǔ doesn't feature any eunuchs but it does star someone who played a significant role in letting them in the back door and consequently bringing down this once great dynasty. Our Chinese Saying this time is Fǔ Dǐ Yóu Yú. I've also seen it written Fǔ Zhōng Yóu yú 釜中游鱼, but most sources go with the Fǔ Dǐ Yóu Yú version.

00:48 | And as we always do, and for very good reason too I might add, let's break down these four characters and see if we can guess the meaning behind today's featured chéngyǔ.

CHINESE SAYINGS BOOK 2
EPISODE 13

00:58	Fǔ Dǐ Yóu Yú.
01:02	A Fǔ is an archaic name of a kind of cooking pot or cauldron.
01:07	Dǐ means at the bottom of. Fǔ Dǐ, at the bottom of the cauldron or cooking pot.
01:13	Yóu means to swim, among other usages.
01:18	And the last character Yú is a fish.
01:22	Now this one is guessable. Cauldron bottom swimming fish. Sounds like some sort of precarious situation. But exactly how precarious and what the situation is, unless you keep a copy of the Hòu Hàn Shū 后汉书, the Book of Later Hàn on your bedside table and are familiar with the chapter entitled Zhāng Gāng Zhuàn 张纲传, chances are you don't know for sure.
01:48	So, the Book of Later Hàn, like all these official histories of the dynasties, was written during the 5th century, during the Liú Sòng Dynasty. But the actual story itself from which we get today's Chinese Saying comes from the Eastern Hàn and stars one of those model officials known for his honesty, integrity, sincerity and decency. His name was Zhāng Gāng 张纲
02:15	He was the eldest son from a well-established family and despite the privileged world he came from, Zhāng Gāng lived a simple and unpretentious lifestyle. He had the misfortune to have lived during a time when the

CHINESE SAYINGS BOOK 2
EPISODE 13

02:37 Eastern Hàn was on its way to extinction, during the reign of young Emperor Shùn 汉顺帝.

This was one of those emperors who left the job of running China to others. His empress was named Liáng Nà 梁妠. She wasn't so bad, but her brother was. And she allowed him to grab hold of the reins of power and he ended up doing all kinds of terrible things that adjusted the trajectory of the Eastern Hàn to a more downward slant. Thanks to the empress's brother, in no time at all Emperor Shùn's imperial court was filled with the most evil, corrupt, self-serving officials. And eunuchs ran amok everywhere making matters much worse.

03:15 So bad did it become that one day Zhāng Gāng exclaimed, "The royal court is filled with wicked, black-hearted men. If I am not allowed to dedicate myself to ridding the country of evil, my life is not worth living."

03:30 In the year 142 at the tail end of Emperor Shùn's reign, the imperial court appointed eight emissaries to travel and report on local affairs within the country. Most of these emissaries were famous noble men, experienced and in high positions in the government, Zhāng Gāng among them. Only Zhāng Gāng, unlike the others, was relatively young and not as high ranking.

03:56 Each of the emissaries travelled to their assigned post, except for Zhāng Gāng, who remained in the capital, Luòyáng, and refused to travel to his assigned region of the country. He said, 'When the imperial court itself is filled with people as vicious, wicked, and violent as wolves, why bother checking on common people who are only as duplicitous, sly, and cunning as foxes?'

04:22   The report which Zhāng Gāng sent back to the emperor contained a tirade that mostly pointed a finger at the Empress's brother, an imperial general of great power named Liáng Jì 梁冀. In that Eunuchs Part 1 episode, I mentioned Liáng Jì. Zhāng Gāng boldly declared that 'The great general Liáng Jì has received countless benefits from the imperial court. However, he is wanton and unfit. Really, he should not be shown any mercy, and should in fact be given the death penalty. Here are fifteen things he has done, which prove that he has not virtuous at all." He proceeded to enumerate the more than a dozen wicked and evil acts that Liáng Jì had carried out or called for.

05:09   This report shocked the entire capital city. Liáng Jì was, by this time, the most powerful person in all of China, not to mention his sister was the empress. Furthermore Liáng Jì's relatives filled the imperial court. Emperor Shùn knew all of this to be true, but he dared not do anything and for Zhāng Gāng's honest report, the emperor ignored him. And this put Zhāng Gāng in the cross hairs of Liáng Jì.

05:38   Meanwhile down in Jiāngsū province in a part of Yángzhōu called Guǎnglíng 广陵, there lived a bandit leader named Zhāng Yīng 张婴, no relation to Zhāng Gāng. And this bandit leader had more than ten thousand men who had been terrorizing those rich lands for more than a decade. Several attempts had been made

CHINESE SAYINGS BOOK 2
EPISODE 13

to get rid of him but Zhāng Yīng could not be beat and his soldiers and fellow bandits operated with impunity in this land.

06:06 Liáng Jì saw an opportunity here and concocted a plan to deal with his accuser Zhāng Gāng. He used his evil ways to arrange for Zhāng Gāng to be appointed the prefect of this seemingly ungovernable and dangerous area. Formerly, officials appointed to this prefecture had always requested heavy military reinforcements from the capital, so unruly and violent was the place.

06:35 But not Zhāng Gāng. He set off with only the lightest military retinue. Once he reached his post in this part of Jiāngsū on the north bank of the Yángzǐ River, opposite the city of Zhènjiāng, he took with him ten or so soldiers, and went directly to the feared bandit leader, Zhāng Yīng's fortress. He announced himself and sought out an audience with Zhāng Yīng in order to appease him and demonstrate the imperial court's mercy and virtue.

07:03 When he stood before Zhāng Yīng he did not show any fear. He earnestly said to him, "The previous prefects who were sent down to deal with you were mostly greedy, violent, and cruel, and tried to force you and your men to band together out of anger to defend yourselves. This was wrong on their part, but your actions, Zhāng Yīng, have also been wrong. Now, the emperor is kind and just, and wishes to convince you and your men to lead upright lives through mercy and virtue. He has sent me here, not to punish you with harsh sentences, but to bring you honor through rewards and positions.

77

Now is truly a good time to turn your sorrows into joy. If you do not take this opportunity of imperial mercy, the emperor, in his anger, might send in an entire army to do away with you."

07:58 He went on to say, "To be unable to correctly assess the strength and weakness of each side involved, that is foolishness; to perform terrible and vicious deeds in the name of truth and beauty, that is stupidity; to give up virtuous obedience for rebellious unruliness, that is bad faith; to risk the lives of your own sons and grandsons, that is unfilial; to stray from the path of goodness in order to follow wicked ways, that is unrighteous; to understand right, but still do wrong, that is cowardly. These six aspects must guide the course of your future and whether you will come to good or ill. I hope you will carefully consider what I have said."

08:47 Zhāng Yīng was profoundly moved by these words and began to weep. He said to Zhāng Gāng: 'We, your humble servants, far removed from the imperial court, have no way of making our grievances heard by the emperor. Unable to bear the oppressions of the corrupt officials appointed to serve here, we banded together out of necessity, and have been scraping a living like this ever since."

09:12 And here is where we get the saying Fǔ Dǐ Yóu Yú. When the bandit leader Zhāng Yīng continued, "Our actions were those of a fish, swimming in a cooking pot, desperate for a few last gasps of air, meaning he and his people were a Fǔ Dǐ Yóu Yú. And then Zhāng Yīng

CHINESE SAYINGS BOOK 2
EPISODE 13

finished off by saying, "Now your words have given me hope for a new life. But now that I have fallen into wicked ways, I worry that we will be ambushed and caught on the day of our surrender."

09:45 Zhang Gang reassured him on this and swore upon the longevity of heaven and earth, and the purity of the sun and moon, that Zhāng Yīng had nothing to be afraid of. Upon hearing these reassuring words, Zhāng Yīng was extremely thankful. After bowing to each other, Zhāng Gāng returned with his men to his camp.

10:08 The next day, Zhāng Yīng brought with him ten thousand men and their wives, all with their hands voluntarily tied behind their backs, symbolically surrendering and submitting to Zhāng Gāng. After words were exchanged, Zhāng Gāng threw a feast for Zhāng Yīng and his men at their fortress.

10:29 Afterwards Zhāng Yīng's gang was disbanded, and all the former ruffians who followed him went wherever they wished. In fact, Zhāng Gāng took it upon himself look after these now, unemployed bandits, granting them land and houses. Those of the bandits who wished to become officials were sure to find letters of recommendation from Zhāng Gāng.

10:52 Following this, everyone was happy and this area at last became peaceful and prosperous. When word reached Emperor Shùn, he at once wished to reward Zhāng Gāng for a job well done. But Liáng Jì wouldn't have it and prevented the emperor from showing any kindness or gratitude on Zhāng Gāng. Instead, the emperor decided to promote Zhāng Gāng and send him to a different area. But upon hearing this, the now former bandit leader Zhāng Yīng as well as his followers, they pleaded with the emperor that he allow Zhāng Gāng to remain as the official in charge of their prefect. And so Emperor Shùn granted their request.

11:37 But only after a year at his post, Zhāng Gāng died at the age of forty-six. Countless people, old and young, showed up at his residence to pay their respects. Ever since Zhāng Gāng had fallen ill, all the people of his prefecture had prayed for him, saying, 'May he live ten thousand years, for when will we come upon such a prefect as this again?'

12:01 Zhāng Yīng and five hundred of his followers dressed themselves in mourning clothes and followed the carriage with Zhāng Gāng's coffin all the way to his burial place in Qiánwéi 犍为, south of Chéngdū in Sichuan province where they themselves helped to bury him.

12:20 Thereupon the emperor passed an imperial edict that said, "The late prefect of Guǎnglíng, Zhāng Gāng, set an example to everyone by his own virtue. By his teachings of honesty and goodness, he pacified the ten thousand people under the great bandit Zhāng Yīng and turned them from evil to good. He calmed the battles and rescued the suffering commoners; but before we were able to promote him, he passed away in his prime. We send our sincere condolences to Zhāng Yīng and all

CHINESE SAYINGS BOOK 2
EPISODE 13

those who mourned Zhang Gang like they would their own father and mother."

12:55 Then the emperor appointed Zhāng Gāng's son, Zhāng Xù 张续 to one of the highest positions in the imperial court and rewarded him as well with riches paid in silver.

13:06 So, a happy ending despite the odds. As for Liáng Jì, if you recall he was the most powerful force in China from 141 to 159. And what a textbook bad guy from Chinese history! Had innocent people killed, ruled through puppet emperors, ruined careers and lives of just and able citizens. He had them all in spades. Anyway, when he killed himself, aside from his relatives who profited from him, not too many tears were shed. And pretty much thanks to this guy, the Eastern Hàn Dynasty fell into a irreversible tailspin and would only last for sixty more years. And that's being generous.

13:52 Okay, Laszlo Montgomery signing off. That's it for season four. A big thanks to all of you for listening and making the CSP one of the top rated Chéngyǔ related history shows out there. Take care everyone.

Chinese Sayings Book 2
Episode 14

MR. GOOD GOOD

好好先生—Hǎo Hǎo Xiānshēng

TRANSCRIPT

00:00 | Welcome everyone Laszlo Montgomery here, with another Chinese Sayings Podcast. This one won't take long.

00:09 | For the season 5 opener, I reserved another good one. Again, a quickie, but one to store in your utility belt as you make you way through life. This one in particular has a nice interesting story attached to it. Actually I thought I did this one already, but when I double-checked the back catalog I realized it only got a quick mention in a past China History Podcast episode. So now I'm giving this great chengyu its due and introducing it to you in this CSP episode.

00:41 | Hǎo Hǎo Xiānshēng. Let's not waste any time and just break it down.

00:46 | Hǎo means good or okay, or yes. So Hǎo Hǎo means good, good or yeah, yeah. When you're talking to people and you say, "yeah, yeah, yeah, uh-huh, yeah." Well, the

CHINESE SAYINGS BOOK 2
EPISODE 14

	Chinese equivalent to that is "haohaohaohaohao". So Hǎo Hǎo is akin to yeah yeah yeah good good.
01:10	And a xiānshēng means Mister.
01:14	So Hǎo Hǎo Xiānshēng means Mr. Good Good. You might be able to guess what this means but this is another one that could mean anything.
01:23	So there's a story attached to this one and it goes way way back to the Eastern or Later Hàn Dynasty, 25 to 220 AD, a certifiably long time ago. And the star of this one is a gentleman named Sīmǎ Huī. 司马徽.
01:40	This story comes to us courtesy of the Gǔ Jīn Tán Gài, 古今谭概 a book of essays written by the late Ming Dynasty literary figure, Féng Mènglóng. 冯梦龙. It's not a particularly famous work. Nor was it the most noted book written by Féng Mènglóng. But it did contain this story about Sīmǎ Huī that yielded this useful Chinese idiom.
02:02	Now, this isn't necessarily true, but in popular Chinese history Sīmǎ Huī is credited, along with Páng Tǒng 庞统, of being the one who introduced Zhūgě Liàng to Liú Bèi. This is all part of Romance of the Three Kingdoms lore. A lot of what was written in Luó Guànzhōng's novel was fiction, including this story. But aside from Sīmǎ Huī's reputation as a hermit and a spotter of talented men, he's not a particularly consequential figure in the history or in the times he lived in.

CHINESE SAYINGS BOOK 2
EPISODE 14

02:34   Now, besides having introduced Zhūgě Liàng to the King of Shǔ, Liú Bèi, one other thing about Sīmǎ Huī that he's remembered for is that, well, he was one of those types who never liked to give anyone any bad news or create waves or anything. Or take sides or possibly upset anyone by saying anything one way or another, about essentially, anything.

02:59   He would go to great lengths to avoid being drawn into any argument or debate and would even go so far as to pretend he didn't understand what was being discussed or asked of him, just to avoid possibly upsetting anyone.

03:15   Whatever anyone asked him, his reply would always be, "hǎo hǎo". If someone asked him how are ya doing, they'd get a "hǎo hǎo". What'd you think of the latest news? "hǎo hǎo". Whadda ya think of this weather, "hǎo hǎo". Even when someone would mention something terrible like there was a death in the family or someone is terribly sick and isn't expected to make it, he'd still retort with a "hǎo hǎo".

03:40   Well, one day Sīmǎ Huī's wife started berating him because a good friend had just visited their residence and had mentioned that his son had passed away. And Sīmǎ Huī replied with the usual "hǎo hǎo". She yelled at him saying, "This poor guy just visited us, no doubt seeking comfort or wise words from you, and all you can say is good good. What's up with that?"

04:04   She went on, "No matter what anyone says to you, all

CHINESE SAYINGS BOOK 2
EPISODE 14

you ever have to say is good good." To which Sīmǎ Huī replied, "Hǎo hǎo".

04:12 So anyone like this who lives their life not to offend anyone and not express their opinions or say anything that might go against whatever the prevailing opinion was being discussed, is a Hǎo Hǎo Xiānshēng. Whatever they're discussing at the moment, it's always a matter of yeah yeah yeah, uh huh, good.

04:32 You know, I've known a few in my lifetime and the last thing a good and decent Hǎo Hǎo Xiānshēng wants to see is someone's raised eyebrow. So this respected but quirky late 2nd century BC figure, Sīmǎ Huī, we remember him for not only his association with Zhūgě Liàng and Liú Bèi, but also as the guy who never wanted to hurt anyone's feelings. So he walked right down the middle of the road and he was neither left nor right, but he was always good.

05:05 Hǎo Hǎo Xiānshēng. Mr. Good Good. Perhaps you have one or two in your life. Doesn't have to be a mister you know. Plenty of Hǎo Hǎo Nǚshì's 女士 out there I'm sure. If you know any of these kind souls out there that I'm talking about, now you have a nice Chinese idiom to ascribe to them.

05:29 And so that is gonna be that for this time. A nice short one for you. I know time is money and your podcast queue is stuffed with episodes so I shan't draw this out any longer than it need me.

CHINESE SAYINGS BOOK 2
EPISODE 14

05:43 | This is Laszlo Montgomery signing off from sunny and beautiful Los Angeles, California. Please consider coming back again next time for yet another interesting and useful chengyu, here at the Chinese Sayings Podcast.

Chinese Sayings Book 2
Episode 15

IT'S TOO LATE BABY !

病入膏肓—Bìng Rù Gāo Huāng

TRANSCRIPT

00:00 | Good evening everybody, welcome back to another useful and interesting Chinese Saying. This is Laszlo Montgomery warmly welcoming you back to the Chinese Sayings Podcast. Chéngyǔ's are us.

00:13 | For this week's offering, coming off the heels of Sīmǎ Huī, the Hǎo Hǎo Xiānshēng, we're back with an oldie from the Golden Age of Chinese Sayings, the Zhou Dynasty, 1046 to 256 BC.

00:28 | And today we travel back the Warring States Period, early 6th century BC to the State of Jìn 晋国, located mostly in today's southern Shānxī Province. And it's specifically during the time of Duke Jǐng that this story takes place. There were two other Duke Jing's of Jìn but they were a different tone and different characters. Duke Jǐng, Jìn Jǐng Gōng 晋景公 reigned there from 599 to 581 BC. One of the other two Duke Jìng's will be the final one to rule Jìn State before it was partitioned a century later into Hán, Zhào and Wèi.

CHINESE SAYINGS BOOK 2
EPISODE 15

01:09 | And our story today comes straight to us from Zuǒ Qiūmíng's Zuǒ Zhuàn 左转. Mr. Zuǒ's Annals which serves as a commentary of the Spring and Autumn Annals attributed to the Great Sage himself, Confucius. This story I'm about to tell you can be found in the chapter entitled Chéng Gōng Shínián 成公十年.

01:32 | Let's break the four characters down, shall we?

01:35 | Bìng 病 means a sickness or disease.

01:39 | Rù 入 means to enter.

01:42 | Gāo 膏 by itself means fat, grease or oil. It can also mean a paste or a cream. However it also has an obscure third definition meaning the vital organs of the body.

01:56 | The character huāng 肓, in Chinese medicine, is the part of the body between the heart and the diaphragm. I'm not sure about today but back in days of yore if you had cancer or any serious ailment in this critical layer in your abdomen, it was curtains for you.

02:14 | So, Bìngrù Gāohuāng. The disease has entered that part of the body that is incurable. I suppose this one sort of gives itself away as far as its potential meaning is concerned. But we can't say for sure. And it's one heck of a story how we got this one.

02:33 | So let's get to the gùshi 故事 behind this Chinese Saying. Like I said, we're in the final year of the reign of Duke Jǐng of Jìn, 581 BC. This Duke, he had one of

90

CHINESE SAYINGS BOOK 2
EPISODE 15

those hateful and malicious concubines who had gone around spreading all these rumors about members of the Zhào family who had been nothing except loyal and supportive of the Jìn royal family going way back.

02:45 One thing about Duke Jǐng was that he had this very hateful and scheming concubine. And for reasons that are not clear, there ended up being two members of this Zhào family in particular, Zhào Tóng 赵同 and Zhào Kuò 赵括 who had somehow earned the concubine's ire. Feeling somewhat miffed and slighted at what these two had said, she went and whispered in the ear of her husband, the Duke, about how these two were up to no good. And she was convincing enough, whereby Duke Jǐng had these two honorable men executed. And not only that, he had their entire families killed as well, the entire Zhào clan.

03:27 As you can imagine, this whole thing was shocking to many people at the royal court. And several of Duke Jǐng's closest advisors asked him how he could do such a thing after so many decades and decades of Zhào family loyalty to the Jìn royal house.

03:44 They must have made Duke Jǐng feel a large degree of remorse because he felt terrible about what he went and did. And to repent, he had one of the sons of a Zhao concubine named as the official heir to the Zhào family name and restored the fortunes of the family by granting this son property and wealth. And in doing so, Duke Jǐng assuaged his guilt about what he did, you know, exterminating the entire Zhào clan.

CHINESE SAYINGS BOOK 2
EPISODE 15

04:14 | Not long afterwards Duke Jǐng had a horrible nightmare where some ghastly spirit with long hair visited him, making a big ruckus and wailing like a banshee. And this being, whatever it was, announced itself as from the Zhào family. And he screeched at Duke Jǐng for killing him and all his sons. And he told the Duke that heaven had granted him the power to choose a punishment to make Duke Jǐng pay for what he had done.

04:47 | The following morning when he awoke, Duke Jǐng had his people summon the royal shaman or witch doctor to interpret what in the heck was the meaning of this horrible nightmare and what actions he should take in the face of such threats. The witch doctor arrived on the scene and as Duke Jǐng began to recount his memories of the nightmare, this shaman or Wū 巫 held up his hand to interrupt Duke Jǐng. The witch doctor eerily recounted in the minutest detail what the Duke had dreamt that night.

05:21 | The Duke cried out, asking what does this mean? How can it be interpreted? The shaman just looked at him and replied, "You will not live long enough to taste the first harvest of wheat next year." Duke Jǐng pleaded with the shaman for more insight and advice on what he should do. But this shaman had nothing further to say.

05:44 | And not very long afterwards, Duke Jǐng began to feel quite ill and knew something was wrong. The next state over to the west of Jìn was Qín. Qín State was mostly in and around Shǎnxī province. They had some doctor of repute there who Duke Jǐng invited to his palace to

CHINESE SAYINGS BOOK 2
EPISODE 15

examine him. So he arranged for this doctor to come to the Jìn capital in southern Shānxī to find out why he was feeling like he was.

06:15 So this doctor rode east towards the capital, and the night before he was scheduled to arrive, once again Duke Jǐng had another horrific dream. This time he was visited by these two bizarre and mischievous childlike spirits. As as they circled the sleeping Duke Jǐng, one said to the other, 'Brother, our host is sending for a good doctor who will do harm to us. He is soon to arrive. How shall we escape him?' The other one grinned malevolently and suggested, 'How would you like to hide with me deep in the membranes above our host's heart?' This was met with a knowing smile. No one would find them there.

07:00 The morning after, Duke Jǐng awoke, shaken from this dream and not knowing what it meant. That same day, the renowned doctor from the State of Qín arrived and was immediately taken to see Duke Jǐng. Upon examining Duke Jǐng, the doctor sighed and said, 'There is nothing I can do. The disease has penetrated so deep that it is lying in between the membrane above your heart. Neither acupuncture needles nor surgical tools will be able to reach it. And it is too potent for any pill or medicine.' He uttered those four characters, bìng rù gāohuāng. The disease had entered his gāohuāng, that part of the body which if afflicted, could never be cured. Not back then anyway.

07:49 With the that strange and terrible dream fresh in his memory Jìn Jǐng Gōng knew the doctor was right. So he

CHINESE SAYINGS BOOK 2
EPISODE 15

sent the doctor away and amply compensated him for his troubles.

08:03 So it was a difficult summer for Duke Jǐng as he lay ill and dreaded the coming of the autumn harvest. And one afternoon when the wheat was harvested, one of his people ceremoniously presented the first harvest to Duke Jǐng. And the Duke didn't feel any worse than he ever did. And he knew right there, that witch doctor was wrong. He said I'd be dead before I could partake of the next wheat harvest. Now it's here before me and, for nothing, I've been stressing out about this.

08:34 The Duke clapped his hands in delight and called for the witch doctor at once. Then he demanded his kitchen staff to grind down the wheat, turn it into flour and prepare him a meal at once.

08:47 Not long afterward, the Wū or witch doctor, he arrived on the scene and faced the Duke in his chambers. And angry Duke Jǐng grimaced and said to the Wū, "You said I wouldn't live long enough to taste the next harvest of wheat. Yet this day has come and I am alive and well and here before me is a bowl of wheat from the first harvest." And for all the mental agony this Wū had caused to Duke Jǐng of Jìn, he ordered him executed at once. And he was frog marched out of there and killed.

09:22 And wouldn't you know it, right at the moment the Duke was about to tuck into this royal dish, he felt a pain in his abdomen that was so great that he knew right away this was it. He was about to die. The sensation in

CHINESE SAYINGS BOOK 2
EPISODE 15

his guts was so painful that he asked to be carried to the water closet. And it was right there on the royal bathroom floor, just like Elvis, the Duke died.

09:51 And indeed, just as the witch doctor had prognosticated he did not live to taste anything from the next wheat harvest. The reason he did not live was because the bìng rù gāohuāng. The disease had already entered his gāohuāng, that part of chest in between the heart and the diaphragm which in Zuǒ Qiūmíng's day was a part of the body that was out of reach of any cure or procedure known to humankind at that time.

10:22 So it's in situations where someone has fallen ill and isn't given long to live and someone asks if there's any hope. This chéngyǔ is used as a kind of euphemism for saying that it's a terminal illness and no cure exists. It's beyond a cure.

10:39 But there's another way this idiom can be used, in a less mortal way to humans. Let's say that your life isn't in danger but you find yourself in a hopeless situation? Bìngrù Gāohuāng. Nothing can save you. Your goose is cooked.

10:55 If some information or damaging images were released on social media that incriminates someone or a company, no matter how they try to contain it, forget it, Bìngrù Gāohuāng. Nothing you can do. It's too late. The damage is done and whatever is gonna happen will happen.

CHINESE SAYINGS BOOK 2
EPISODE 15

11:22	If relations between countries or between certain ethnic groups gets so out of hand and acrimonious that no amount of contrition or diplomatic negotiations can save it, give up. It's over between those two. Bìngrù Gāohuāng. It's beyond the point of salvation and nothing can be done to make it better.
11:43	So no matter you're using this saying in the context of a fatal illness or in a hopeless situation where nothing can save you, Bìngrù Gāohuāng. The disease has penetrated the Gāohuāng, that part of your anatomy where you don't want to experience any dreaded disease.
12:00	I hope no one has to ever use this one anytime soon but just the same, you might hear someone else utter this one day. So now you're completely wise to the story behind this great chéngyǔ that, as I said, comes to us direct from the Chronicles of Zuǒ Qiūmíng, known as the Zuǒ Zhuàn.
12:21	And on behalf of everyone here at the main office in Los Angeles, California, this is Laszlo Montgomery wishing you all the very best and inviting each and every one of ya's to come back next time for another exciting episode of the Chinese Sayings Podcast.

Chinese Sayings Book 2
Episode 16

BE ALL THAT YOU CAN BE

投笔从戎—Tóu Bǐ Cóng Róng

TRANSCRIPT

00:00 | Welcome back everyone to another Chinese Sayings Podcast. Laszlo Montgomery here once again with another chéngyǔ for your ever-expanding collection.

00:12 | Why it took five seasons to finally get to this one I'll never know. Tóu Bǐ Cóng Róng. 投笔从戎. I was thinking that this one perhaps didn't have too much of a practical usage out in the real world. But then again, although it wasn't the most relatable Chinese saying, the story behind it was of such historical interest I figured, I gotta tell it. Plus I have a few CHP listeners who would probably relate to this one.

00:41 | But before we go and do all that, let's break down these four characters that make up this chéngyǔ, Tóu Bǐ Cóng Róng.

00:48 | Tóu means to throw, fling or hurl something.

00:53 | And a bǐ is a pen. Tóu bǐ, to throw the pen.

CHINESE SAYINGS BOOK 2
EPISODE 16

00:58 | Cóng has a whole slew of meanings, but the one relevant to this Chinese saying means to join or be engaged in.

01:06 | And Róng means military affairs or a military campaign. Cóng róng, to join the military.

01:15 | Throw down the pen and join the military. I'm sure everyone's got some idea about this one.

01:21 | So let's dive into this story, that tale is chock full of Hàn Dynasty history.

01:27 | We start with an illustrious man named Bān Biāo who is immortalized as the one who wrote the Book of Hàn, the Hàn Shū, the second of the Twenty-four official histories. This Book of Hàn chronicled the people and events of the Western Hàn Dynasty.

01:48 | The Hàn Shū was so well written and put together, it became a model for all future official histories written by each dynasty about the dynasty that they had just succeeded. So it was during the Eastern Han that the official history of the Western Hàn was written. Later on, there will be the Hòu Hàn Shū or Book of Later Han, that will be published during the succeeding Liú Sòng Dynasty. That's how it worked with these things.

02:17 | Bān Biāo started the Book of Han, but it was his son Bān Gù 班固 and his daughter Bān Zhāo 班昭 who would complete the work and achieve renown equal to that of their eminent father. And this father Bān Biāo shared a similar fate with historian Sīmǎ Tán who came before

CHINESE SAYINGS BOOK 2
EPISODE 16

him. Both would begin a great and momentous work of historiography. But they would both die before their job was done. And it fell to their children to complete it, or to the one son in the case of Sīmǎ Qiān and the completion of the Records of the Grand Historian.

02:54 Some of you perhaps recall mention of the Bān family from the Part 3 episode of that epic twelve-part History of Xīnjiāng series from early 2020. This son was named Bān Chāo. He was the son of Bān Biāo and brother to Bān Gù and Bān Zhāo.

03:16 Bān Chāo is remembered as a strategist of the highest order and famous for winning a lot of battles despite often being far outnumbered or in the less advantageous position militarily. He's remembered and lionized in Chinese history for the fight he led out in Xinjiang for thirty years, warring with the Xiōngnú and restoring the Tarim Basin to Hàn China control. Bān Chāo's military and diplomatic achievements saw him extend Hàn China influence beyond Xinjiang, as far west as the Caspian Sea.

03:52 That's where Bān Chāo made his mark in Chinese history. But before all that happened, he was following in the footsteps of his father and siblings and worked as a historian as well. But he had no passion for this subject except when he would occasionally come across the stories of Fù Jièzǐ 傅介子 and Zhāng Qiān 张骞.

04:13 He was moved by the actions and accomplishments of those two in particular. Fù Jièzǐ, during the time of Hàn

CHINESE SAYINGS BOOK 2
EPISODE 16

Emperor Zhāo 汉昭帝 carried out a secret mission that ended in the assassination of the King of Lóulán in 77 BC and the planting of the China flag in Xīnjiāng. And Zhāng Qiān of course, who I covered in CHP episode 47, whose mission to the Western Regions, called for by Hàn Emperor Wǔ 汉武帝, led to the eventual opening up of that part of Central Asia and the launching of the Silk Roads that did so much to change China and so much of Asia.

04:54   As Bān Chāo toiled in the library with his brother and sister, bored out of his mind at the work he was doing, he was inspired by the achievements of these two Western Hàn Dynasty greats and dreamed of following in their footsteps. He so admired them for their contributions in improving the Han Empire's political relations with regions to its west and fortifying the Han Empire's Western border. Bān Chāo vowed that someday, he too would do something great for his country.

05:26   As he toiled away in Luòyáng as a court scribe, alongside his brother and sister he finally got fed up and threw down his writing brush. In other words, he tóu bǐ, and declared, "Real men should be out winning honor like Fù Jièzǐ and Zhāng Qiān, laying down their lives for the country in distant lands! How can one toil away year after year in matters of brush and ink?"

05:55   So right then and there, Bān Chāo threw down his pen, or he tóu bǐ, and made up his mind to cóng róng, to join the army. His colleagues at the library who heard Bān Chāo utter these words mocked him and told him he was crazy.

CHINESE SAYINGS BOOK 2
EPISODE 16

But like the young lad from the old chéngyǔ from Season Three that told the story of the Hónghú zhī zhì 鸿鹄之志, Bān Chāo exclaimed, "How can people with no foresight or direction understand the ambitions of a man of virtue?"

06:28 Thereupon Bān Chāo left behind this life of the scholarship that had won his family so much acclaim, though with little of financial benefit to show for their work. And by 73 AD Bā Chāo, through his skills and ambition, had risen high up in the Hàn military ladder. And in today's Hāmì 哈密 Prefecture at Barkol Lake he won a stunning victory over the Xiōngnú and proved himself to be not only a great warrior but a brilliant tactician as well.

07:00 And I can't not say this, but this daring military victory over the Xiōngnú was immortalized in the well-known Chinese Saying that I haven't covered yet in the CSP: Bùrù hǔxué yān dé hǔzi 不入虎穴焉得虎子, you can't catch the tiger's cubs without entering the tiger's lair. Or Nothing ventured, nothing gained, as we say in English, borrowing from the 14th century French proverb "Qui onques rien n'enprist riens n'achieva."

07:30 Following this victory over the Xiōngnú, Bān Chāo's talent was recognized and he went on to become one of the most successful military leaders of his age. And not only Bān Chāo, the Bān family's renown carried forward another generation when his son Bān Yǒng continued in his father Bān Chāo's footsteps in serving the Han Empire out in present day Xinjiang.

CHINESE SAYINGS BOOK 2
EPISODE 16

07:55   And just as Bān Chāo one day declared when he tóu bǐ cóng róng, when he threw down his pen and joined the military, many years later he joined the great Fù Jièzǐ and Zhāng Qiān as both a general and a diplomat who through his conquest and diplomacy flew the China flag in those far western regions that so many others who followed him would conquer and retreat from over the course of China's long history.

08:23   So this is a chéngyǔ that perhaps not many of us can relate to unless one of you walked away from a life of a desk job and chose instead to be all that they could be, in the army. But for those who listened to the call, and like Bān Chāo before them, tóu bǐ cóng róng, turned their back on their lives that they believed had no meaning and opted to join the military, a Chinese saying from two thousand years ago.

08:52   Tóu bǐ cóng róng. That's the story behind that one. The Book of Later Han and the chapter Bān Chāo Lièzhuàn. It's all in there, including this four character saying.

09:03   Okay, that, I'm afraid is gonna have to be it. The editorial and production staff here tell me to keep these CSP episodes in the five to eight minute sweet spot but sometimes I ramble. Not so bad this time.

09:19   On behalf of all the other helpers, hangers on and Apple Scruffs, this is Laszlo Montgomery signing off on a sunny Los Angeles day with snow on the mountains behind a backdrop of palm trees, I cordially invite every single one of you to come back next time for another

CHINESE SAYINGS BOOK 2
EPISODE 16

entertaining and informative episode of the Chinese Sayings Podcast.

 Chinese Sayings Book 2
Episode 17

MAKES NO DIFFERENCE

九牛一毛—Jiǔ Niú Yī Máo

TRANSCRIPT

00:00 | Hi Everyone, me again, Laszlo Montgomery. Another day another chengyu. And I'm happy to bring you, once again, another staple from the annals of great Chinese Sayings. This chéngyǔ was even used by the late great James Clavell, mentioned in Noble House if I recall correctly. Maybe Tai-Pan also, who knows. This one's useful in all kinds of situations.

00:26 | And as usual only four characters involved. Our Chinese Saying is Jiǔ Niú Yī Máo. And without any further wasting of precious time, before we commence the telling of the story, allow me break it down for you. Jiǔ Niú Yī Máo.

00:43 | Jiǔ is the number nine.

00:46 | Niú means an ox or a cow. Jiǔ Niú, Nine oxen.

00:52 | Yī is the number one.

CHINESE SAYINGS BOOK 2
EPISODE 17

00:55 | And Máo, aside from being the character for Chairman Máo, it also means a feather, or fur or hair in this case. Yī Máo, one hair.

01:06 | Nine Oxen One Hair. Well, well what could that mean? Jiǔ Niú Yī Máo. Let's go find out.

01:14 | From a document called Bào Rén Shàoqīng Shū 报任少卿书, we get this well-worn classic story that stars none other than the Grand Historian Sīmǎ Qiān himself. We remember him of course for his achievement in completing the great work started by his father, The Record of the Grand Historian, the Shǐ Jì. And if not for this text written way back in the Hàn Dynasty, there would be a lot of blank spaces in the annals of Chinese history going back to the beginning.

01:49 | This story takes place during the time of one of China's greatest emperors. The Hàn Emperor Wǔ, Hàn Wǔdì. This martial emperor had a major hand in stretching China's borders out beyond the traditional Yellow River valley and its tributaries. He did this mainly through conquest and to a lesser extent by diplomacy.

02:10 | One of his generals was named Lǐ Líng 李陵. He had done well as a Hàn general and worked his way up the military ladder. During the early part of Emperor Wǔ's fifty-four year reign from 141 to 87 BC, he had decided, after so many incursions into Hàn China by the marauding Xiōngnú, that it was high time to hit back against them.

CHINESE SAYINGS BOOK 2
EPISODE 17

02:35 The Xiōngnú are often referred to in the history books as the Huns. But they were a tribal confederation who thrived on the Mongolian Steppe, north of everything happening along the Yellow River and the Central Plain of China. They had been a stone in China's boot for a long time and Emperor Wǔ made up his mind to once and for all, push them back north and out of these lands bordering China.

03:03 General Lǐ Líng was ordered to provide backup support for the great general Lǐ Guǎnglì 李广利 who was given overall command in dealing with these fierce nomads of the steppe. Lǐ Guǎnglì was a favorite of Emperor Wu thanks to his sister being the emperor's favorite concubine.

03:21 Lǐ Líng was kind of hoping to get his own command and had spoken up too soon and overconfidently about all the damage he'd be able to do on his own with only 5,000 crack troops. He said he'd deal decisively with these Xiōngnú barbarians and to just leave it to him.

03:41 To make a long story short, the emperor gave him the okay and even though he knew it was risky and that he probably shouldn't have acted so cocky, Lǐ Líng rode off towards the Tiānshān Mountains. That's the chain that runs north of Xinjiang, running to the west into Kyrgyzstan and Uzbekistan.

04:00 Well, Lǐ Líng sort of walked right into a buzz saw. He had expressed too much optimism to the emperor as far as how easy it was gonna be to give the Xiōngnú

CHINESE SAYINGS BOOK 2
EPISODE 17

a lickin'. When he encountered the Xiōngnú army he found himself grossly outnumbered. And even though he hung in there a while and inflicted a great amount of pain and suffering on the Xiōngnú army, in the end, he was soundly defeated and captured by the Xiōngnú.

04:31 The way it worked in those days, when you got an order direct from the emperor and you failed, you had best fall on your sword because your career was, for all intents and purposes, over.

04:43 Instead of killing himself Li Líng opted to defect and lived out the rest of his days amongst the Xiōngnú and helped train their military. When word got back to Hàn Wǔdì about the loss in battle, he was livid to say the least. And reading the emperor's mood correctly, all of Lǐ Líng's detractors at court piled on and dissed him in front of the emperor and everyone took turns putting their sword into Lǐ Líng.

05:11 And while everyone at the palace was giving their two cents to the emperor and painting Lǐ Líng's defeat in the worst possible light, Sima Qian stood by silently, not saying anything. Li Líng had always been a friend and political ally of his. So he opted not to stick a knife in his back.

05:32 The Han Emperor Wu turned to Sima Qian and asked his illustrious palace historian what did he think about this whole thing. Well, he should have just gone along with what everyone else was saying because it was pretty evident Lǐ Líng was cruisin' for a bruisin' with

CHINESE SAYINGS BOOK 2
EPISODE 17

Han Wudi over the whole defeat. The emperor hadn't heard yet about the defection. That came later. And when he found out, the emperor would order the summary execution of Lǐ Líng's wife and mother. That was a harsh unforgiving time back then.

06:05 Sima Qian instead of going with the flow, defended Lǐ Líng and said even though he fell to the Xiōngnú he had always served well in the past and had many victories under his belt. He continued that Lǐ's army of 5,000 faced off against tens of thousands of Xiōngnú mounted soldiers. True he had been annihilated but he had lasted more than ten days in battle and had killed thousands more of the Xiōngnú. He even said they shouldn't discount the notion that perhaps he willingly surrendered so that he might regain his strength and when the time was right, avenge the country and conquer the Xiōngnú.

06:49 Sima Qian had even inferred in a roundabout way that Emperor Wu's favorite, Lǐ Guǎnglì, hadn't fared too well against the Xiōngnú either and once he let that slip out, that was it. The Emperor put his foot down and charged Sima Qian with insulting the royal person with his remarks. The penalty was a fine that Sima Qian, at his annual salary, could hardly afford to pay. So he was given the option to be executed or be castrated and serve three years in prison.

07:23 Yeah, not a particularly attractive couple of choices. As Sima Qian sat in his jail cell he contemplated his fate. His friends came by to visit him and tried to offer solace.

 CHINESE SAYINGS BOOK 2
EPISODE 17

07:37 | He told one of his closest colleagues that it remained of paramount importance that he complete this great historical work he had been working on, the as yet unfinished Records of the Grand Historian, the Shǐ Jì.

07:53 | He came to the realization that if he died before finishing this work that his father Sīmǎ Tán had begun, his disgrace would be even greater than the castration. Without completing this work, aside from disgracing his father's memory, his death would be as meaningless and insignificant as the loss of a single hair from a total of nine oxen. Jiǔ Niú Yī Máo. It was a drop in the bucket.

08:22 | If his life was like a single hair from an ox, it meant his death would be as significant as the loss of one hair from the back of an oxen. It would have absolutely no impact whatsoever on the way the world turned. He would die, failing to leave his mark and his whole life would have been utterly meaningless and forgotten in no time. Like a single hair lost from nine oxen.

08:50 | So Sima Qian, China's most respected and renowned historian from ancient times went through with the castration and lived out the rest of his life as a eunuch in the imperial palace. They weren't terribly respected in the palace hierarchy though many of course attained stratospheric amounts of power and wealth. So Sima Qian carried on with his work, stigmatized by this public shame he carried wherever he went because of the particular punishment meted out to him for his verbal transgression.

CHINESE SAYINGS BOOK 2
EPISODE 17

09:26 | But on the other hand here we are almost two thousand years later and his fame and renown, at least in China and with those who study China, is still very much alive and celebrated. And had he allowed himself to be executed, he never would have finished the great work for which he is immortalized. We would have no memory of him and, indeed, his life would have been worth no more than a single hair from nine oxen. It wouldn't have mattered.

09:57 | And whenever you want to show something is quantitatively insignificant, a drop in the bucket as we say using the English idiom, of no importance, you can say it's nothing more than a single hair taken from nine oxen. Utterly useless. Something no one would miss. To express the magnitude of anything as being utterly insignificant and too small to even count for anything, you can use Jiǔ Niú Yī Máo. Works every time.

10:29 | And that's all I have for you today. Jiǔ Niú Yī Máo, a single hair from nine oxen. A classic Chinese Saying if there ever was one. And made even more memorable because the backstory for this chengyu concerns the great Sima Qian, one of the patron saints I may add of the CHP, The China History Podcast. Hundreds of hours of programs covering Chinese history from mythical times to the present day.

11:06 | Well, that's a gonna be it. Take care everyone. This is Laszlo Montgomery wishing all ya'lls the very best and encouraging you to come back next time for another practical episode of the Chinese Sayings Podcast.

Chinese Sayings Book 2
Episode 18

DARN MULBERRY TREE!

指桑骂槐—Zhǐ Sāng Mà Huái

TRANSCRIPT

00:00 Welcome back ladies and gentlemans, Laszlo Montgomery here bringing you another season of Chinese Sayings, curated by us, for you. We have ten beauties all lined up for you in this sixth season of this podcast show that seeks to offer you some of the great stories behind some of the well-known and not so well-known Chinese Sayings. And over the next twenty weeks you'll get to hear them all.

00:27 And for the Season Six opener, I have the pleasure of offering up another one of my all-time favorites. I say that a lot because I have quite a few all-time faves and this is one of them. Many of you have heard it before. But how about the story behind it?

00:39 Oh yeah? You know the story? Well, which one, because for our season opener you're going to get two versions behind today's featured Chinese Saying for the price of one.

CHINESE SAYINGS BOOK 2
EPISODE 18

00:50 | Zhǐ Sāng Mà Huái. Let's break this one down.

00:56 | Zhǐ means a finger if it's a noun and it means to point if you use it as a verb.

01:02 | A Sāng is a white mulberry or just a mulberry tree. Morus alba, the botanical species that is associated with the silkworm, perhaps the most important animal species in China's commercial history.

01:16 | Mà means to verbally abuse, curse, swear, call names. You get the idea.

01:23 | And a huái is a species of tree called a Japanese Pagoda tree. Sophora japonica. It's also known as a Chinese scholar tree or a Zuì Huái 罪槐, or Guilty Scholar tree. This might ring a bell because of the famous specimen planted in Jǐngshān Park behind the Forbidden City Beijing that the Ming Chóngzhēn Emperor used to hang himself on that sad day back in 1644. And I'm not sure why, since it's a different species, but a huái is also known as a locust tree and you can check Pleco on that if you want.

02:05 | Point Mulberry Tree Scold Locust Tree.

02:09 | Let's not guess what this means. Instead we'll go straight to the original usage of Zhǐ Sāng Mà Huái. And this comes to us straight out of the Thirty-Six Stratagems, the Sānshíliù Jì 三十六计.

02:22 | This book, along with Sūnzǐ's 'Art of War' make up

CHINESE SAYINGS BOOK 2
EPISODE 18

China's two most famous ancient works of military strategy. These Thirty-six Stratagems worked not only on the field of battle, but in politics and everyday relationships and situations.

02:38 The thirty-six strategies themselves can be traced back to the Southern and Northern Dynasties of 420 - 598 A.D. There are Six chapters to the book, containing six stratagems each. The first three chapters of the thirty-six strategies are referred to as 'winning' strategies, or strategies one might employ when they're in an advantageous position. The last three chapters are 'losing' strategies, or strategies reserved for when you're operating from a disadvantageous position, such as when your city has been surrounded by enemy troops.

03:20 Our Zhǐ Sāng Mà Huái saying for this time comes from the last half of the book that explains how commanders were to deal with internal conflict within the ranks. Although the Thirty-Six Stratagems were passed down through the centuries, they were only formally edited and collected into a book sometime during the Ming or Qing dynasties. The Thirty-Six Stratagems gives this example of a famous general using the Zhǐ Sāng Mà Huái 指桑骂槐 strategy:

03:50 The star of our tale is Tián Rǎngjū 田穰苴 also known as Sīmǎ Rǎngjū. He's been compared to Jiāng Zǐyá 姜子牙 who you no doubt recall from China History Podcast Episode 258. Tián Rǎngjū lived during the long reign of Duke Jǐng of Qí, 547 to 490 BC. Spring and Autumn Period. Tián Rǎngjū was quite the talented man who sought refuge in the Kingdom of Qí after his own kingdom was invaded and destroyed.

04:48 The Kingdom of Qí, present day Shāndōng province, had been suffering a series of defeats and the ruler Duke Jǐng wanted to shake things up within the army by hiring some new generals. Someone recommended Tián Rǎngjū to him. After interviewing him, the Duke of Qí was very impressed and immediately offered him command of a whole army.

04:51 But Tián Rǎngjū wasn't born yesterday and said to Duke Jǐng, 'My lord, I don't come from the nobility of this country. I'm worried that if you put me, a commoner, in charge of military officials and an army, no one will obey my commands. I suggest that you appoint a trusted official as my co-commander so that people will respect our collective authority.'

05:15 The Duke of Qí saw the wisdom of this statement and appointed one of his favorite officials, Zhuāng Jiǎ (庄贾), as Tián Rǎngjū's co-commander. Tián Rǎngjū immediately went to Zhuāng Jiǎ's house to inform him. The two agreed that they would meet at noon the next day at the army camp to take over command.

05:35 Now Zhuāng Jiǎ, as a powerful official, had lots of friends in high places. He wanted to celebrate his promotion to commander, and his friends insisted to throw him a farewell party. So, early the next day, Zhuāng Jiǎ's friends all showed up at his house and started making merry. Zhuāng Jiǎ drank bowl after bowl of wine and

CHINESE SAYINGS BOOK 2
EPISODE 18

ignored his servants' urgent reminders that it was time to depart for the military camp.

06:04 Meanwhile, Tián Rǎngjū had arrived well before their appointed meeting time of noon. He had already organized some of the camp's affairs and set out new patrol times. Then, he had all his soldiers get into formation, ready to depart the camp and set off to war. When Zhuāng Jiǎ didn't arrive at noon, he sent someone to inquire after Zhuāng Jiǎ. To pass the time productively while waiting, he began to drill the soldiers.

06:34 The messenger from the camp arrived at Zhuāng Jiǎ's house to hurry him. But Zhuāng Jiǎ was at the height of his merrymaking and was annoyed by the messenger. "Go away! New commanders always take things too seriously. What's a few more minutes?" Saying this, he sent the messenger away.

06:55 After Tián Rǎngjū finished drilling the soldiers, Zhuāng Jiǎ had still not appeared. Tián Rǎngjū arranged the soldiers in formation again, ready to depart, and sent another messenger to Zhuāng Jiǎ. By this time, all the men at Zhuāng Jiǎ's house were well and truly drunk. Zhuāng Jiǎ saw another military messenger and slurred, "Not another one! Tell him we'll be done in a minute."

07:20 At the military camp, the sun was setting. Another messenger arrived to tell Tián Rǎngjū that his army was needed quickly, since there was an enemy invasion at a nearby town. Tián Rǎngjū decided to go himself to get Zhuāng Jiǎ. Just as he was mounting his horse,

CHINESE SAYINGS BOOK 2
EPISODE 18

Zhuāng Jiǎ, so drunk that he was swaying on his feet, staggered into the camp. Tián Rǎngjū was furious and asked Zhuāng Jiǎ where he had been. Zhuāng Jiǎ said, "Oh, just drinking with a few friends who came to send me off. It's no big deal."

07:59 Tián Rǎngjū began to berate Zhuāng Jiǎ: "The day a military official receives his command, he should forget his obligations to his colleagues and friends. By the time he has arrived at camp, he should forget his duty to his father and mother. By the time the battle drums sound and he rides into war, he should forget even his instinct to save his own life. The Kingdom of Qí faces enemy invasions every day, and even the Duke of Qí himself can barely eat or sleep from worry. Just in the last few hours, we've received news that another town is under attack. How can a general even think of farewell drinks at such a time?"

08:39 He summoned an officer in charge of martial law and asked him, "How do we deal with a soldier who is late to his post?"

08:46 The officer said, "The penalty for lateness is death."

08:51 Zhuāng Jiǎ panicked and immediately sent someone to the Duke of Qí to plead for his life. But Tián Rǎngjū was not about to wait for the Duke of Qí to send word back. He had already wasted too much time that day. Without further ado, he had Zhuāng Jiǎ dragged to the middle of the camp, where everyone could see, and sliced off his head.

CHINESE SAYINGS BOOK 2
EPISODE 18

09:12 | Almost as soon as Zhuāng Jiǎ's head rolled off his shoulders, an emissary from the Duke himself barged into the camp at top speed in a horse-drawn carriage, causing great disorder among the soldiers. "The Duke says not to behead Zhuāng Jiǎ!" panted the emissary.

09:29 | Tián Rǎngjū replied to him, "As a military general appointed in a time of emergency, I have the right to judge what is done in my own camp." He then turned to the martial law officer and asked, "What is the penalty for someone who disrupts the camp by driving horses into the soldiers?"

09:47 | "The penalty is death," said the officer.

09:51 | "I cannot behead one of the Duke's own emissaries," said Tián Rǎngjū, "but to teach him a lesson, his footmen shall be killed, and his carriage broken." So in front of everyone, the emissary's footmen were beheaded and one side of the carriage was smashed.

10:07 | Now everyone knew that Tián Rǎngjū was not to be trifled with. Seeing that their general was so determined, no one dared to even think about stepping out of line. Tián Rǎngjū, leading the most well-disciplined army in China, was easily able to drive out the invaders. By publicly berating and punishing Zhuāng Jiǎ and the emissary, he had shown the whole army that he was a general to be feared and respected.

10:38 | In the Thirty-Six Strategies, the annotation to the strategy of 'Pointing at the Mulberry while Cursing the Locust Tree' is: '大凌小者, 警以诱之. 刚中而应, 行险为顺.' Dàlíng xiǎozhě, jǐngyǐ yòuzhī. Gāngzhōng ér yīng, xíng xiǎn wéi shùn, 'Control those under you by providing a suitable deterrent for bad behaviour. Demonstrating an appropriate amount of force can turn a precarious situation into an advantageous one'. It's also been translated as, "In order to discipline, control, or warn others whose status or position excludes them from direct confrontation; use analogy and innuendo. Without directly naming names, those accused cannot retaliate without revealing their complicity."

11:25 Now the other and much more popular version concerning the provenance of Zhǐ Sāng Mà Huái comes to us courtesy of Cáo Xuěqín's classic novel 'Dream of the Red Chamber'. From the story of Tián Rǎngjū we can see how Cáo applied 'Pointing at the Mulberry while Cursing the Locust Tree' to express misdirected anger.

11:48 In the Dream of the Red Chamber version, Zhǐ Sāng Mà Huái is used by these old household servants who express their petty discontent toward the master by complaining about another household servant whom the master favored. They dared not risk any backlash or counterattack by openly and directly complaining about someone. Instead, they pointed to someone else and by making this remark. It's clear what they really meant.

12:16 But if you do employ the Zhǐ Sāng Mà Huái tactic and someone hits back at you, well, you still have a small fig leaf covering your plausible deniability. And if you're like some people I know, and I won't name names, you

CHINESE SAYINGS BOOK 2
EPISODE 18

can actually counterattack by denying what you said isn't what you meant, even though it was. This one, Zhǐ Sāng Mà Huái, if you're in a relationship with anyone, you gotta be vigilant because you might be a victim one day, or victimize someone else.

12:47 Point at the mulberry tree and scold the locust tree. Used in cases where a direct verbal attack leaves you exposed in the event of any pushback. So rather than directly making your caustic remarks to the one intended, you criticize something or someone else who can stand in as a proxy to make your point clear. You know and the stand-in for the mulberry tree both know who you're talking about. But if they say, hey man, what the...! You can immediately raise your hands and say, hey dude, I'm not talking about you, I'm talking about that locust tree over there.

13:23 Yeah, I don't know about the frequency with which this particular Chinese Saying is used. But the act described in Zhǐ Sāng Mà Huái, especially the Dream of the Red Chamber version, gets used in all kinds of life situations. All embracers of the science of passive aggression keep this one in their utility belt for occasional use.

13:47 Okay, that's gonna be it my friends for Episode one of this new season. Nine more good ones coming, I assure you. This here's Laszlo Montgomery once again signing off from the sunny and baking hot draught-stricken climes of Los Angeles, California. Do consider coming back again next time for another story behind a useful and interesting chengyu, here at the Chinese Sayings Podcast.

Chinese Sayings Book 2
Episode 19

THE GREAT REJUVENATION

多难兴邦—Duō Nàn Xīng Bāng

TRANSCRIPT

00:00 | Hello again my friends, good to see you again, Laszlo Montgomery here welcoming you to the Chinese Sayings Podcast. Thanks for tuning in and listening. Another quickie today. I know you're busy.

00:14 | Today we look at duō nàn xīng bāng. This is a Chinese Saying that perhaps people in many countries might find relevant to their situation. But let's not waste time with any further chitter chatter and get down on it.

00:28 | Duō nàn xīng bāng. And the breakdown four characters:

00:32 | Duō means many, much or more.

00:36 | And Nàn means difficult, hard or a calamity or misfortune.

00:42 | And Xīng means to prosper, rise, prevail or become popular.

CHINESE SAYINGS BOOK 2
EPISODE 19

00:47 | And the character Bāng is just another way to say a nation or country.

00:52 | And when you string those four characters together, you get duō nàn xīng bāng. Many hardships revive nation. And just hearing those words, you can pretty much guess correctly what the meaning is behind this chéngyǔ. Not terribly difficult to figure out.

01:09 | But as I've been preaching since Season 1, it's not enough to know what these characters mean, you gotta know the story behind it. And then you can nod your heads sagaciously next time you hear it or read it and truly appreciate its significance.

01:24 | And for the story behind this chéngyǔ, we need to go back all the way to the Warring States Period, to the Zuǒ Zhuàn, The Commentary of Zuǒ, a work that is believed to have been written by one Zuǒ Qiūmíng 左丘明. The Zuǒ Zhuàn is for the most part a commentary on the Chūnqiū or Spring and Autumn Annals, attributed to Confucius, The Great Sage.

01:46 | And this story dates back to the 6th century BC, to the year 545, the time in the Eastern Zhou dynasty known as the Spring and Autumn period, a period when the Zhou Dynasty kings were still reigning but not ruling. Beginning in the 8th century BC, it was every duke and king for himself.

02:10 | As I mentioned, our story dates back to 545 B.C. when the King of Chǔ down in the Húběi Húnán region, King

CHINESE SAYINGS BOOK 2
EPISODE 19

Kāng 楚康王, died. And like all these Chǔ kings, he was surnamed Xióng. Chǔ's main enemy was the State of Jìn based mostly in southern Shānxī, as well as Wú to the east of Chǔ, where the Yángzǐ River emptied out into the East China Sea.

02:36 King Kāng's son Xióng Jūn 熊麇 inherited the throne. Xióng Jūn immediately promoted his uncle, Prince Wéi 公子围, and relied on him as one of his most valuable advisors. But Prince Wéi had a bit of a slime factor and while he served his nephew, he only had his own best interests at heart. Soon, he began plotting to murder Xióng Jūn and make himself the new king of Chǔ.

03:03 Four years later, in 541 B.C., Prince Wéi's opportunity came. That year, Prince Wéi was sent on a diplomatic mission to the Kingdom of Zhèng. But soon after he set off, he received word that his nephew, Xióng Jūn was seriously ill. Prince Wéi abandoned his mission and hurried back to the palace. And as soon as he was alone with his nephew, because he was so weak from his illness, Xióng Jūn could not resist when his uncle put his hands around his neck and strangled him. And in order to prevent any of Xióng Jūn's sons succeeding him, Prince Wéi killed both of them.

03:42 Of course, this act of brazen cruelty did nothing to endear Prince Wéi to the palace ministers who were all wise to the murder. But Prince Wéi was determined to seize power and nothing was going to stop him, and he had the most vocal of his political enemies at court murdered.

CHINESE SAYINGS BOOK 2
EPISODE 19

03:59 | The Prince of Wéi's own two brothers fled the country and defected to the kingdoms of Jìn and Zhèng. And with the greatest opposition to his usurpation now dead or living in exile, Prince Wéi had himself declared King Líng of Chǔ 楚灵王.

04:16 | At this time in China history, the Kingdoms of Chǔ and Jìn were the two most powerful of the Warring Kingdoms. And Chǔ and Jìn regularly took turns to host summits between all the kings of the warring states. In 538 B.C., the new King of Chǔ, King Líng, he wanted to host this year's summit in order to cement his position. He thought that if he could display his power amongst all the other rulers, it would silence the voices of dissent within his own realm. So King Líng sent an emissary to the Kingdom of Jìn with his request to host the summit.

04:54 | But the ruler of Jìn, Duke Píng 晋平公, he also wanted to host this summit. He was very reluctant to accede to the ambassador's request. But rather than make a whole scene, he showed no emotion and very politely told the ambassador to go and rest, since he must be tired. Duke Píng immediately summoned his most trusted advisor, Sīmǎ Hóu 司马侯, to discuss the matter.

05:19 | Sīmǎ Hóu asked Duke Píng what he wanted to do. Duke Píng said, "Jìn is a stable country with a strong military and an able government. The Kingdom of Chǔ is full of internal troubles. What right does this usurper King Líng have to demand that he host this summit? Chǔ is a mess and he cannot even take care of his kingdom's own affairs." Thereupon Duke Píng told Sīmǎ Hóu he was

CHINESE SAYINGS BOOK 2
EPISODE 19

going to decline the King of Chǔ's request.

05:48 But Sīmǎ Hóu replied, "If this is your grounds for denying the King of Chǔ's request, it is not very well thought out. History shows that a stable and prosperous country often becomes careless and loses power. On the contrary, if a country has suffered in recent years, its people are often more united and more patriotic. Their shared suffering will enhance the people's spirit of solidarity. And this will soon help the country to prosper again.

06:18 "Look at Duke Héng of Qí 齐恒公. In 685 B.C., Duke Héng's predecessor was murdered, and the Kingdom of Lǔ took this opportunity to invade Qí. But Duke Héng quickly took control and easily beat back the Lǔ army. His victory made his country strong and very soon, the Kingdom of Qí became the first of the Hegemons of the Spring and Autumn period.

06:43 "And if you want an example from your own country, look at Duke Wén of Jìn 晋文公. Duke Wén was exiled and unable to take power. This led to great internal strife within Jìn. But as soon as Duke Wén finally returned, after all the hardship there, the Kingdom of Jìn had a period of rejuvenation and went on to become the second Hegemon of the Spring and Autumn period.

07:09 "So, Your Majesty, you cannot rest your hopes for dominance on the internal troubles of the Kingdom of Chǔ. In fact, based on what we know of the King of Chǔ's wanton and narcissistic personality, if you grant him

CHINESE SAYINGS BOOK 2
EPISODE 19

this little concession, mark my words, he will become too proud and arrogant and will fly too close to the sun and this will cause his own downfall. Then with King Líng out of the way, who will be left to vie with you for the position of head of the annual summit?"

07:39 Duke Píng of Jìn immediately saw the wisdom of Sīmǎ Hóu's words. He sent for the ambassador from Chǔ and agreed that the summit should be held in the Kingdom of Chǔ that year. And just as Sīmǎ Hóu had predicted, the King of Chǔ's ego became so inflated by this position that he became even more unpopular than before. The summit turned out to be a great failure because of his unbearable attitude. All the rulers from the various states were completely turned off by his arrogance. King Líng then stopped holding court with his own ministers. His two brothers, who had fled when he first took power, took this opportunity to attack and seize the throne. And in the end, King Líng of Chǔ was forced to commit suicide by his own brothers in 529 BC.

08:29 And from Sīmǎ Hóu's wise words to the Duke of Jìn, we get the saying: Duō Nàn Xīng Bāng... 'Many hardships may strengthen a nation'.

08:40 So to describe a phenomenon where, when a nation suffers many hardships and calamities, they display a spirit of unity and patriotism that eventually helps them to rise again and regain their lost prosperity. And when that happens, you don't want to mess with them.

CHINESE SAYINGS BOOK 2
EPISODE 19

08:58 | What better example exists than in China where after a hundred years of suffering at the hands of predatory nations during the 19th century and into the early 20th, the people, in all their misery found strength and unity in their abysmal state and experienced a great rejuvenation. Duō Nàn Xīng Bāng.

09:19 | And maybe today, in places that are in a sorry state due to a whole range of political and economic crises, Venezuela, Zimbabwe, Sudan, South Sudan, Syria, Somalia, maybe for them too, Duō Nàn Xīng Bāng. These hardships they face today, let us hope they can find strength in this period of suffering to revive the nation.

09:45 | Duō Nàn Xīng Bāng. Much distress regenerates a nation. Calamity in the country prompts a renewal.

09:55 | And there you have it my friends, the penultimate episode for this Season 6 of the Chinese Sayings Podcast. Just one more to go before I take my between seasons break and rejuvenate myself.

10:09 | This is Laszlo Montgomery signing off once again from the wilds of Los Angeles, California, beseeching all of you to consider coming back next time for otro emocionante episodio del Chinese Sayings Podcast.

**Chinese Sayings Book 2
Episode 20**

AS CLOSE AS LIPS N'TEETH

唇亡齿寒—Chún Wáng Chǐ Hán

TRANSCRIPT

00:00 | Welcome back ladies and gentlemans to another season of the Chinese Sayings Podcast. This is the seventh season of this ultra-niche podcast show that, may I remind you, my naysayers said would pod-fade in no time at all. Still alive and kicking.

00:18 | And for the Season 7 opener do I ever have a good one for you! All imbibers of early PRC history know this one I'm sure. And no less a personage than Chairman Mao himself, uttered today's four character Chinese Saying, Chún Wáng Chǐ Hán. Chairman Mao thought this was was so apropos, he used it himself back in the day. And Máo Zédōng, if you can say nothing else about him, he knew his chéngyǔ's. Even invented a few himself.

00:49 | But The Great Helmsman wasn't the first one to use this ancient Chinese idiom. To find where it originated, you'd have to thumb through your copy of the Zuǒ Zhuàn, The Chronicles of Zuǒ that detailed the history of Eastern Zhou China from 722 to 468 BC. The Spring

CHINESE SAYINGS BOOK 2
EPISODE 20

	and Autumn Period. That's where Chún Wáng Chǐ Hán comes from.
01:12	Before we begin the story behind this four syllable Chinese Saying, let's first look at the characters that make up the idiom: Chún Wáng Chǐ Hán.
01:21	Your Chún is your lip.
01:24	And Wáng means lose or be gone, among other definitions. Chún Wáng, the lips are gone.
01:32	And a Chǐ is a tooth.
01:35	Hán means cold.
01:39	And when you join all four characters together you get: lips gone, tooth cold. Not much of a clue. Therefore in order to figure this idiom out all we can do is check out the backstory from whence it came.
01:51	So let's climb into our wayback machine and set the dials for the 650's BC. And our story takes place in the mighty State of Jìn at a time when Jìn was riding high as the most powerful and consequential of the early Eastern Zhou Era states. Co-starring in this story are the much smaller and mostly forgotten states of Guó 虢国 and Yú 虞国. These two Dukedoms went all the way back to the beginning of the Western Zhou and were both located very close to the Zhou ruling family, both politically and geographically.

CHINESE SAYINGS BOOK 2
EPISODE 20

02:26   Like Guó and Yú, the State of Jìn also went way back to King Chéng, the son of the Zhou Dynasty co-founder, King Wǔ. King Chéng was famously looked after during the period of his minority by his Regent the Duke of Zhou. So these states, all close to the King, all right near each other on the map, and all three were descended from the royal Jī family who founded and ruled the Zhou Dynasty.

02:56   Yú and Guó, these two recognized their precarious situation, being small states bordering a giant like Jìn. So these two stuck together and always had each others' back. And up to now, there hadn't been any major incidents.

03:14   During the reign of Duke Xiàn of Jin, Jìn Xiàn Gōng 晋献公 676-651 BC, the Duke of Guó couldn't contain his aspirations to expand his state and grow his power. Often he would order his troops to attack and harry the borders of Jìn.

03:33   Duke Xiàn of Jìn was outraged at these attacks coming from Guó to his south. And he wracked his brain trying to come up with a way to respond to such provocations. But nothing came to mind. At last, Duke Xiàn went to his trusted advisor, Xún Xī 荀息, and asked him: "Can't we just perform some kind of a special military operation to attack the State of Guó and then annex it?"

04:00   Xún Xī replied, "Don't consider that option, your highness, unless you want to entangle yourself in a two-front war with Guó and Yú. Those two states are so close that you can't invade Guó without Yú coming to its aid, and we can't be confident that our forces are a match for their combined military power."

04:21 Duke Xiàn sighed and said, "Then I guess our only option is to stand by and do nothing as our borders are constantly harassed by Guó forces." Xún Xī replied, "Not exactly. I know that the Duke of Guó is easily distracted by beautiful women and losing himself to the pleasures of the flesh. I suggest that you send him a gift of a number of beautiful Jìn women and you mark my words, in no time at all he'll forget duties of state. And with his eye off the ball, so to speak, poor governance will soften them up and make Guó nice and ripe for an invasion."

05:01 Duke Xiàn thought this was an interesting notion and did exactly as Xún Xī suggested. After everything was arranged and sent some veritable beauties down to Guó, just as Xún Xī had predicted, the Duke of Guó soon let matters of state fall to the wayside as he lost himself to the pleasures of this gift from Duke Xiàn of Jìn.

05:25 Seeing this, Duke Xiàn began calling for his Jìn forces to prepare to invade Guó. But when Xún Xī heard about this he came straight to Duke Xian at once and said, "Not so hasty your highness. You've weakened Guó, but we still need to think of a way to prevent Yú from coming to Guó's aid.

05:44 "I happen to know that the Duke of Yú is a man who treasures short-term gains over long-term profits.

CHINESE SAYINGS BOOK 2
EPISODE 20

Because of this, I humbly suggest you make him a gift of all your most precious jades and your best horse, and in return for this gift, you then ask him for easy passage through Yú to attack Guó. Listen to me when I say Duke of Yú will not deny you."

06:10 Duke Xiàn said, "That'll never work. For one thing, I'm not sure that I would give up my most precious jades and my best horse just to defeat the State of Guó. I mean, it's such a small territory. Not to mention, the ruler of Yú will know for sure that I had just sent all those beautiful women to Guó. Won't it seem strange that we offer him such extravagant, and in fact, priceless gifts and then suddenly ask for safe passage to invade Guó?"

06:40 Xún Xī said, "As for your first point, you wouldn't really be giving up your jades and your favorite horse. If Guó falls, Yú is sure to follow. The two states have survived this long only because of each other's mutual aid. So when Yú falls, you will get your jades and your horse straight back.

07:00 "And as to your second point, why, that's also easily resolved. Send a squad of men to go raid and harass Guó's borders with Jìn. I guarantee you Guó's border officials will come straight here and will start berating you for allowing this. Then you'll have a convenient excuse to tell the Duke of Yu and that you wish to invade Guó to punish them for insulting you."

07:25 And, Duke Xiàn did exactly as Xún Xī advised, and sent a few men to cause trouble on Guó's borders. Just as

135

CHINESE SAYINGS BOOK 2
EPISODE 20

Xún Xī predicted, Guó sent emissaries to criticize Duke Xiàn. Thereupon, according to the plan, Duke Xiàn sent Xún Xī, along with his most precious jades and his best horse, to the State of Yú.

07:47 When Xún Xī was able to get an audience with the Duke of Yú, he first presented Duke Xiàn's fine horse and precious jades. The Duke of Yú almost couldn't believe the rarity and fineness of the gifts he had just been handed. He asked Xún Xī: "Why has Duke Xiàn sent these gifts to me? These are famous treasures of your Jìn state, and much too fine to part with."

08:14 Xún Xī replied, "My master wishes to ask a favour of you. The State of Guó has often caused unrest along our southern borders and recently insulted Duke Xiàn besides. My master wishes to punish them for their actions, and the easiest way to invade Guó is through your Yú state. Thus, I have been sent to ask for safe passage for the Jìn armies to march through Yú on their way to Guó. If by good luck we succeed in our mission, any bounty we capture will be, of course, shared with you."

08:47 At this point, according to the words written in the Chronicles of Zuǒ, the Duke of Yú's advisor, Gōng Zhīqí, drew him aside. "Sir," he said, "you cannot grant Duke Xiàn's request under any circumstances. The states of Guó and Yú are like lips and teeth. Now there is a saying among the common folk that goes, Chún Wáng Chǐ Hán. 'If the lips are cut off, the teeth will be cold." Guó is like the lips in this analogy, and we are the teeth. If they are harmed, harm will surely come to us."

CHINESE SAYINGS BOOK 2
EPISODE 20

09:22 The Duke of Yú replied, "Jìn is clearly sincere in their intentions, or they would not have sent us such priceless treasures. Even discounting the quality of their gifts, would it not be better to have a powerful friend like Jìn instead of a weak one like Guó?"

09:39 No matter how much Gōng Zhīqí remonstrated with him, the Duke of Yú's eyes kept straying to the beautiful jades and the noble steed. And after silently calculating their estimated worth, his mind was firmly made up to grant Jìn's request. Gōng Zhīqí knew that this meant the death of the state of Yú, so that night he packed his bags, took his entire family with him, and fled the region.

10:06 In 655 BC, the state of Guó was indeed annexed by the state of Jìn. And just as Xún Xī had promised him, a portion of the spoils of their conquest were sent straightway to the state of Yú, with a polite request to station their army in Yú just a little longer so that the tired soldiers could rest before continuing on to Jìn.

10:30 Without the benefit of Gōng Zhīqí's sober judgement, the Duke of Yú happily granted this request. And to no one's surprise except his own, the Duke of Yú's state fell to Jìn immediately after, and following this conquest, sure enough, just as Xún Xī had said, the Duke of Jìn was able to reclaim all the precious gifts he had given to Yú.

10:53 So this Chinese Saying is used to describe any kind of relationship that is so close that when one party suffers, the other does too. It can be used in an international relations context as well as an interpersonal context.

CHINESE SAYINGS BOOK 2
EPISODE 20

11:10 | This story also gave rise to the Chinese saying Jiǎ Tú Fá Guó 假途伐虢 that is right out of the Thirty-Six Stratagems. Borrow the resources of an ally to attack a common enemy. Once the enemy is defeated, use those resources to turn on the ally that lent them in the first place.

11:30 | And during the Korean War, when Kim Il-sung sent out an urgent SOS to Chairman Mao, the Great Helmsman knew, in this fight, the PRC and North Korea were as close as lips and teeth. And if the Imperialists knocked out Kim Il-Sung, the lips in this example, the teeth, meaning China along the North Korean border, will get cold. And for this reason Mao had Marshal Péng Déhuái throw everything he had at the American-led forces. There is some dispute about who Chairman Mao called the lips and who was the teeth, but you catch the drift.

12:05 | This quote from Máo Zédōng was translated in the press using the phrase "as close as lips and teeth". But what the good Chairman actually said was Chún Wáng Chǐ Hán, if the lips are gone, the teeth get cold. We're all in this together. We have common cause. United we stand, divided we fall. If one of us is defeated, the other's sure to follow. This chéngyǔ is used to describe any interdependent diplomatic relationship where the stress suffered by one state will be felt by the other due to their closeness and interdependence.

12:45 | And like I said, you can also use this in describing alliances between people.

CHINESE SAYINGS BOOK 2
EPISODE 20

12:51 | Chún Wáng Chǐ Hán, if the lips are gone, the teeth get cold. And that, mes amis, is gonna be it for the season opener. Nine more coming over the next eighteen weeks.

13:03 | Okay, one down nine more to go. That's it for episode one of this Season Seven of the Chinese Sayings Podcast. Laszlo Montgomery here signing off from the town they call the city of Los Angels. And I am cordially inviting each and every one of you to come back again next time for another thought-provoking and useful chéngyǔ, here at the Chinese Sayings Podcast.

Chinese Sayings Book 2
Episode 21

I WANT YOU TO SHOW ME THE WAY

老马识途—Lǎo Mǎ Shí Tú

TRANSCRIPT

00:00 Welcome back all chengyu and China history lovers, Laszlo Montgomery here for the ninth time this season, with one more Chinese Saying for your collezione.

00:11 I'm guessing most Chinese speakers have at least heard of this one. Lǎo Mǎ Shí Tú. The old horse recognizes the way. That's what those four characters say, but that's not necessarily what they mean.

00:24 So once again, to get the backstory, we'll have to turn to the great ancient and medieval classics from all the superstars of their day and locate our copy of the Hán Fēizǐ, and take that one off the shelf to get the story behind these four characters.

00:41 But before we do that let's see what these four characters mean.

00:45 A lǎo mǎ is an old horse. Yeah, another Chinese Saying with a horse. Second time this season.

CHP CHINESE SAYINGS BOOK 2
EPISODE 21

00:53 | To shí means to know or to recognize. This character comes in a second and fourth tone version. I'm not sure why but all my Chengyu books assure me in this case it's second tone.

01:07 | And a tú 途 is a road or route or way.

01:11 | And line these characters up in a row and they say Old Horse recognizes the way. Simple enough but let's go to the story and the meaning.

01:20 | Let me first mention this one co-stars someone so esteemed, so sacred and important in ancient Chinese history and culture, even The Great Sage himself, Confucius, he had said of this man, "Had it not been for Guǎn Zhòng, we would all be wearing our hair loose, and our robes folded on the left!" Confucius pointed to this person and said thanks to Guǎn Zhòng's reforms, all of those future generations would now enjoy an orderly and harmonious society.

01:54 | Guǎn Zhòng was an advisor to the most consequential of rulers to govern the State of Qí. This was Duke Huán.

02:01 | This story takes place in Yān State, today, basically the Beijing Municipality area. Way before Beijing became Beijing, first it was the State of Yān.

02:14 | In the Yān (燕) Mountain Range in today's Hebei and Beijing area, there were two small kingdoms: Lìngzhī (令支国) and Gūzhú (孤竹国). The ancient Lìngzhī state was situated just west of Tángshān, in fabulous

CHINESE SAYINGS BOOK 2
EPISODE 21

02:35 | Héběi Province. And Gūzhú was located next door and stretched east to the Bóhǎi Sea.

These mountain people who originally inhabited those two states were an ancient ethnic group called the Shānróng 山戎族.

02:44 | These two ancient territories that could trace their history all the way back to the Shāng Dynasty, were well-protected by the impenetrable forests and twisting valleys of the Yān Mountains (燕山). Outsiders often referred to these two places as the Mountain Kingdoms.

03:01 | For decades, the Mountain Kingdoms had been coordinating attacks on their larger neighbors to the south and to the east. This was back in the 7th century BC so, given the state of technology and engineering, these rulers in Lìngzhī and Gūzhú felt secure in knowing that their own home bases were all but immune to counterattack.

03:22 | But in the spring of 663 A.D., when the famous Duke Huán of Qí received word from the Duke of Yān that the Mountain Kingdoms had once again invaded Yān, he decided that he had had enough. He declared that he would personally lead a Qí force into Yān territory to help Yān defeat their antagonizers. So he set out from Qí and among his retinue was none other than the very Guǎn Zhòng I just told you about.

03:53 | Duke Huán led the combined Qí and Yān armies on a successful campaign against the mountain kingdom of Lìngzhī. His forces utterly destroyed them. The shattered remnants of the Lìngzhī army, along with the Duke of Lìngzhī, were forced to retreat into the lands of the other mountain kingdom of Gūzhú. They made their way to the palace and this defeated duke of the now former Lìngzhī begged for Gūzhú's help.

04:24 The Duke of Gūzhú knew with Lìngzhī knocked out, the Mountain Kingdoms were now quite vulnerable and he knew, left to his own devices, it was doubtful he'd be able to continue to keep the Qí and Yān armies out of the Yān Mountains.

04:39 At this point, one of the Duke of Gūzhú's advisors told him that there was no way he could defeat the Qí and Yān armies. They told him that he should consider parlaying with Qí and Yān and to try and work something out. Another advisor chimed in and and said that, in addition to cutting the best deal for themselves, they should also offer to execute the Duke of Lìngzhī, who, as I said, was now a refugee in Gūzhú. The advisor further said if they offered to bring them the head of the Duke of Lìngzhī's, you know, it might soften them up a little and demonstrate Gūzhú's sincerity.

05:13 The Duke of Gūzhú thought about this. Killing the Duke of Lìngzhī was no problem. But he wasn't quite ready to admit defeat. He replied to his advisors, "Our small army might put us at a disadvantage, but you underestimate the topography of our Yān Mountain range. This terrain gives us a fighting chance against Qí and Yān."

CHINESE SAYINGS BOOK 2
EPISODE 21

05:40 | After discussing the matter at length with his advisors, they came up with this plan: one of his chief advisors, a man named Huáng Huā 黄花, was instructed to go to the Qí and Yān armies and pretend to be a defector from Gūzhú. He was to say that Gūzhú was in complete disarray, with the whole kingdom and all its people wanted to make peace with Qí and Yān.

05:59 | And to embellish the story Huáng Huā was to mention how the Duke of Gūzhú was refusing to admit defeat. Huáng Huā was to beg Qí and Yān to lead their armies into Gūzhú to get rid of the unpopular monarch. And most important, Huáng Huā had to offer to act as their guide.

06:20 | However, this was all a ploy to lead the armies of Qí and Yān astray in the Yān Mountains, where they would undoubtedly get hopelessly lost and disorganized. To give strength to this false story, the Duke of Gūzhú had the Duke of Lìngzhī executed anyway, and gave his head to Huáng Huā as a token of peace. With the Duke of Lìngzhī's head in hand, Huáng Huā hurried to the Qí and Yān army camps, where his story was told and was immediately believed.

06:49 | The combined armies fell into line at once and followed Huáng Huā who led them deeper and deeper into the Yān Mountains, pretending to be taking them to Gūzhú. But one morning, Duke Huán of Qí woke up to discover two facts: firstly, that Huáng Huā had pulled a moonlight flitting, and secondly, that he and his army were now hopelessly lost somewhere in the Yān mountains.

CHINESE SAYINGS BOOK 2
EPISODE 21

07:16 Now their first objective was to find their way back out of the mountains and into Qí. But try as they might, the army could not navigate its way out. They had come to invade the mountain kingdoms in spring, and now it was winter. Thick snow covered the terrain, and it looked completely different from when they had first come.

07:38 Just as the army was getting truly despondent, Duke Huán's advisor Guǎn Zhòng spoke up. He said, "Your Highness, May I make a suggestion. It's my belief, that perhaps the old horses can be of some use to us in our predicament." Duke Huán listened to Guǎn Zhòng's plan and agreed at once. Thereupon Guǎn Zhòng ordered the soldiers to choose the oldest horses in the army, and to unbridle them and allow them walk free.

08:06 The most senior among the horses at that desperate hour, sniffed the air, looked around and started walking. The soldiers were instructed to follow the old horses. And sure enough, they began setting a steady pace, without wavering, and the old horses led the army southward out of the mountains and back to their pleasant home in Qí.

08:30 And when the Duke of Qí reached the edge of the mountain range and first saw the plain before him, he knew he had dodged this bullet. And he further knew, as Hán Fēizǐ said in his classic eponymous work, Lǎo Mǎ Shí Tú. The old horse knows the way.

08:47 And if you were wondering what ever happened to Gūzhú? Well, for their treachery, leading Duke Huán and the forces he led astray to perish in the Yān Mountains,

CHINESE SAYINGS BOOK 2
EPISODE 21

Duke Huán went back a few years later in 660 BC and put an end to to their perfect little world and that was the end of the Gūzhú State.

09:07 So, Lǎo Mǎ Shí Tú. The old horse knows the way is a metaphor to describe experienced people who are familiar with all kinds of life situations and can be called upon in times of need to play a guiding role.

09:23 It doesn't matter what kind of metaphorical old horse it is. Someone in your community, a retired senior executive who knows how to pull companies back from the brink. An old government official. Anyone who has been around the block a few times and has a lot of experience in a particular field or activity. Lǎo Mǎ Shí Tú. This old horse knows the best way to approach and navigate through some crisis or life situation successfully.

09:54 Sometimes there's no substitute for experience. When you find yourself or your company up the creek without a paddle, remember Lǎo Mǎ Shí Tú. Sometimes that old horse will come to the rescue and lead you to victory or help you achieve your aim.

10:12 Okay, Lǎo Mǎ Shí Tú… next time you get lost in the mountains, you may want to keep that one handy.

10:18 All right, that's all's I got for you this time. Sorry I can't drag this one out any longer. This is Laszlo Montgomery signing off on a lovely spring day here in Los Angeles, imploring you to consider coming back next time for another exciting episode of the Chinese Sayings Podcast.

 Chinese Sayings Book 2
Episode 22

GIMME THREE STEPS

退避三舍—Tuì Bì Sān Shè

TRANSCRIPT

00:00 Welcome back everyone, glad to see you tuning in. Laszlo Montgomery here with another Chinese Sayings Podcast. And like pretty much every single Chinese Saying presented on this podcast feed since 2016, this one too is rooted in history.

00:17 And today's chengyu, Tuì Bì Sān Shè, doesn't disappoint. This one comes to us courtesy of The Commentaries of Zuǒ, the Zuǒ Zhuàn. This is one of the more well-known stories from these Warring States times. But before we get to it, let's look at the four characters that make up the Saying.

00:35 Tuì Bì Sān Shè.

00:38 Tuì means to move back or to retreat.

00:41 And Bì means to avoid or evade.

00:45 Sān is the number three and Shè means a house or a

shed or hut. But it also has an archaic usage that means a distance of 30 li which is about 15 kilometers or 9.3 miles.

00:59 So Move back, avoid three shè. Three Shè would be ninety lǐ or about 45 kilometers or 28 miles.

01:08 No hint there about what this might mean. So let's get to the story. A good one from the Warring States Period concerning the Kingdoms of Jìn and Chǔ. And the headliner of our story is none other than Chóng'ěr, who one day became the heroic Duke Wén of Jìn.

01:25 This famous story from the 7th century BC begins with Chóng Ěr's father, Duke Xiàn of Jìn. He was a warrior and during his long twenty-six year reign he made a lot of conquests and expanded the size and might of Jìn State. In 672 BC he defeated one of the barbarian Róng tribes. And among the many spoils of war Duke Xiàn took, were two sisters from these Róng people, named Lí Jī 骊姬 and Shào Jī 少姬

01:52 There were so many femme fatale's of this late Bronze Age in China and Lí Jī, Concubine Lí, she was among that loathsome aggregation. She was known as the Yīdài Yāo Jī 一代妖姬, the Witch of the Age because of her devious acts.

02:09 Now I don't want to step on any toes over at the China History Podcast so let's just cut to the chase about what all went down between the years 657-651 BC. The backstory to this is one of the most popular themes in all of Chinese history, lasted all the way to the end of

CHINESE SAYINGS BOOK 2
EPISODE 22

the Qing Dynasty in the 20th century. And that was, the scheming royal concubine trying to kill the crown prince to get her own son on the throne.

02:36 Duke Xiàn of Jìn 晋献公, was he ever enamored by these two sisters Lí Jī and Shào Jī. And Lí Jī, she had a son with Duke Xiàn named Xīqí 奚齊. And both sisters used their easy access to Duke Xiàn to convince him to get rid of his two sons, the crown prince Shēnshēng 申生 and the star of our tale Chóng'ěr.

02:59 The crown prince, he got all tangled up in a conspiracy conceived by Lí Jī and he ended up killing himself. So she made fast work of the crown prince. And then she turned her sights on Chóng Ěr. Meanwhile she was able to get her son, Prince Xīqí onto the Jìn throne. But not for long. He'll get bumped off a month later.

03:19 Upon Lí Jī's urging, Duke Xiàn sent out orders to arrest his second son, Chóng Ěr 重耳. But Chóng Ěr got wind of these events and fled Jìn before his father's forces could catch up to him. For the next nineteen years, this prince endured a life of hardship and exile from his Jìn homeland. Chóng Ěr traveled around the Warring States of 7th century BC China, going from kingdom to kingdom.

03:47 In a rare period of respite from his wanderings, Chóng Ěr once found himself in the powerful Kingdom of Chǔ, one of the hegemons of the Warring States period. There, he was granted an audience with King Chéng of Chǔ 楚成王.

**CHINESE SAYINGS BOOK 2
EPISODE 22**

04:01 | Even though Chóng Ěr was exiled and down on his luck at the time, the King of Chǔ saw that he was a talented and ambitious man, and predicted that he would go on to accomplish great things one day. Thus, he hosted Chóng Ěr handsomely at the Chǔ court, treating him like a visiting prince.

04:19 | One day, the King of Chǔ threw a banquet in Chóng Ěr's honour. Over the course of the festivities, the king asked him, "If you ever return to Jìn and regain the kingdom that is yours by right, will you repay me for all the kindness and generosity I have shown you during your stay in my kingdom?"

04:36 | Chóng Ěr replied at once, "Your Majesty, with what can I repay you? You possess a bounty of beautiful women, slaves, jewels, and fine silks. As for rare birds and feathers, ivory and precious animal skins, the Kingdom of Chǔ is renowned everywhere in China for these. What can a lowly state like Jìn offer the King of Chǔ?"

05:00 | The king said, "Be that as it may, how would you repay me for my kindness in hosting you during this time?" Chóng Ěr thought for a moment and replied, "If, owing to the kindness of friends such as yourself, I am able to return to rule over Jìn, I vow to remain allies with your kingdom of Chǔ. If our armies ever cross swords, I vow to retreat for ninety lǐ first, to give your army the advantage, before engaging."

05:28 | Remember ninety lǐ was equal to 3 shè which was equal to about 45 kilometers. So now you know where this

CHINESE SAYINGS BOOK 2
EPISODE 22

chengyu is going.

05:37 In a few short years, with the help of Duke Mù of Qín who had also hosted Chóng Ěr, indeed this exiled prince was able to resume his rightful place as ruler of Jìn. This was in 636 BC.

05:51 And it was Chóng Ěr who is also remembered as the capable and wise Duke Wén of Jìn, Jìn Wén Gōng 晋文公. And thanks to the policies enacted during his reign from 636-628 BC, the state of Jìn grew to become the most powerful among all the Warring States. But mighty Jìn would began its decline in the 6th century BC and ultimately suffer the historic Partition of Jìn in the 5th century that divided the land into the new states of Zhào, Hán and Wèi.

06:20 So we can see where this chengyu comes from, the promise Chóng Ěr gave to King Chéng of Chǔ. Chóng Ěr swore if they ever met on the field of battle, in recognizing the kindness he once showed to him, he'd have his army Tuì Bì Sān Shè. He would Tuìbì, he'd withdraw and move out of the way, sān shè, three shè or once again, about forty-five kilometers. And this would allow Chǔ to gain an advantage if the two sides met on the battlefield. And in doing thusly, Chóng Ěr, now the Duke of Jìn, would have honored his promise to King Chéng of Chǔ.

06:50 Well, one day, in 633 A.D., this indeed came to pass that the armies of Chǔ and Jìn met in battle. To fulfill his vow to King Chéng of Chǔ made so many years ago, Duke

CHINESE SAYINGS BOOK 2
EPISODE 22

Wén of Jìn ordered his forces to Tuì Bì Sān Shè, retreat for sān shè or ninety lǐ from the Chǔ army.

07:13 | The Chǔ army seemed to be unaware of the promise that Duke Wén had made to King Chéng. The Chǔ generals watched the Jìn forces retreating three shè and misinterpreted this, believing they were retreating out of fear. Therefore the Chǔ army became overconfident and pressed on, full speed ahead, believing they had the Jìn soldiers on the run.

07:34 | But this was a disorganized attack, launched too quickly, before they were fully ready to mount such an operation. Thus, the Jìn army was able to defeat Chǔ in battle, ironically because of Duke Wén's promise during his exile.

07:50 | So this Chinese Saying Tuì Bì Sān Shè has come down to us to mean, figuratively, to avoid conflict, often with positive connotations of 'beating a strategic retreat'. You're not running away. You're just ensuring you can survive to fight another day.

08:08 | So, no matter at your place of employment, at a board meeting of your condo, in an argument with your partner or loved one, or if you're a politician. Sometimes it's better to Tuì Bì Sān Shè before you act too rashly or not think something through.

08:25 | And so, there it is. Our thanks once again for Zuǒ Qiūmíng 左丘明 for giving us that one. The Commentaries of Zuǒ the gift that keeps on giving...for chengyu's anyway.

CHINESE SAYINGS BOOK 2
EPISODE 22

08:38 | Well, that's going to be it for now. Laszlo Montgomery here signing off from baking hot Los Angeles, California and thankfully not Phoenix. Better get used to this weather everyone. Think about coming back next time, and it won't be long, for another informational episode of The Chinese Sayings Podcast.

 Chinese Sayings Book 2
Episode 23

RUN FOR YOUR LIFE

项庄舞剑, 意在沛公—Xiàng Zhuāng Wǔjiàn, Yìzài Pèigōng

TRANSCRIPT

00:00 | Welcome ladies and gentlemans to another episode of the Chinese Sayings Podcast. This is Laszlo Montgomery here with the fourth offering I have for you in this Season 8.

00:12 | This one's gonna take some time, but it's another great 3rd century BC story that was handed down to us by Sīmǎ Qiān, El gran historiador. This one comes from the chapter Xiàng Yǔ Běn 史记：项羽本. Chronicle of the life of Xiàng Yǔ.

00:27 | This is one of those eight character chengyu's. Four plus four. We haven't had one of those since Sài wēng shī mǎ, yān zhī fēi fú in Season 6. Quite a stellar cast in this story. Lucky Liú Bāng and Xiàng Yǔ, and I'm not talking about the rapper from Taiwan either. The real Xiàng Yǔ. And the third big name is Liú Bāng's trusted advisor Zhāng Liáng 张良. He was one of the Hàn Chū Sān Jié 漢初三傑, the Three Heroes of the Early Hàn Dynasty. Hán Xìn 韩信 and Xiāo Hé 萧何 being the other two.

01:01 | Before we go any further lets break this eight syllable chengyu down into its constituent parts. Xiàng Zhuāng Wǔjiàn, Yìzài Pèi Gōng. Oooh, that's a mouthful. Okay, the first two characters Xiàng Zhuāng 项庄. That's a person name. He was both a close advisor and a relative of the Chǔ King Xiàng Yǔ. And a Wǔjiàn 舞剑, that's a sword dance. You can also say Jiànwǔ 剑舞. A jiàn is a sword and wǔ is to dance. You've seen these, these sword dances are something that are part of traditions all over the world, in Africa, Asia and Europe. And in China sword dances are a one of the many manifestations of Chinese culture. You can see them often in Chinese opera.

01:49 | So Xiàng Zhuāng Wǔjiàn, Xiàng Zhuāng sword dance. Then the next four characters Yìzài Pèi Gōng. Yìzài means to intend to or intended to. And the final two characters Pèi Gōng, that's another person's name. Before Liú Bāng became the founding emperor of the Hàn Dynasty, one of his titles was the Duke of Pèi, Pèi Gōng.

02:14 | The Duke of Pèi was a little inside joke of Liú Bāng. He came from a place called Pèi County 沛县 just to the north of Xúzhōu 徐州 in northwest Jiāngsū province. No one gave him that title. He just gave it to himself.

02:28 | So when you line everything up, we get Xiàng Zhuāng sword dance, intention the Duke of Pèi. Hmmm, sounds dangerous, but without knowing the following story, this one is kind of a head scratcher.

CHINESE SAYINGS BOOK 2
EPISODE 23

02:41 So this one takes time to tell so let's get right to it. Anyone familiar with late Qín early Hàn history and especially the Chǔ Hàn Contention 楚漢相爭, you know this story inside out from 206 BC of The Banquet at Hóngmén 鸿门宴.

02:57 If you recall from past episodes, in 206 B.C., rebel forces led by Xiàng Yǔ overthrew the Qín Dynasty at the Battle of Jùlù. As the majority of the Qín army was engaging Xiàng Yǔ's great army at Jùlù, the Qín capital of Xiányáng was left poorly defended.

03:17 A smaller rebel contingent led by Líu Bāng, the Duke of Peì, seized this opportunity to enter and occupy Xiányáng, that's modern day Xīān.

03:27 At this juncture, a spy within Líu Bāng's forces sent a message to Xiàng Yǔ, telling him: "The Duke of Peì is scheming to take over China. With the region of Guānzhōng, including the capital of Xiányáng, in his control, he will install the last Qin Emperor, Zǐ Yīng (子婴), as his prime minister. All the riches of the area will be his."

03:52 Guānzhōng, which translates to "between the passes" is one of the historical regions of ancient China. It's located in the centre of today's Shǎnxī Province, including the cities of Xiányáng which was later called Cháng'ān. This plain is surrounded by four mountain passes, Hángǔ 函谷关 in the east, Wǔ 武关 in the southeast, Xiāo 萧关 in the northwest and Dàsǎn Pass 大散关 in the west.

CHINESE SAYINGS BOOK 2
EPISODE 23

04:16 | I've been watching the great drama series Dà Qín Dìguó, and these mountain passes are mentioned often and were always crucial to the defense of the Qín State and later Empire.

04:27 | Xiàng Yǔ was furious that Liu Bang had pulled a fast one like this. He ordered his forces to prepare to set out the very next day to crush Líu Bāng's army. At the time, Xiàng Yǔ commanded four hundred thousand troops from his base at Hóngmén, also known as Swan Goose Gate. Líu Bāng had perhaps only a quarter the troops of Xiàng Yǔ.

04:50 | Xiàng Yǔ's advisor, Fàn Zēng 范增, said to Xiàng Yǔ: "When the Duke of Pèi was at home in Shāndōng, he was a greedy and lustful man, thinking only of riches and concubines. Now that he has occupied Guānzhōng, he has given up all thought of wealth and women. From this you can see that he is serious in his ambition. I have also sent men to observe the skies over his base, and they speak of clouds shaped like dragons and tigers, such as appear when a new Emperor is about to be crowned. My lord, you must strike now before the Duke of Pèi becomes more powerful!"

05:26 | Now Xiàng Yǔ's uncle, Xiàng Bó 项伯, was good friends with an advisor in Líu Bāng's army named Zhāng Liáng. When Xiàng Bó learned of Xiàng Yǔ's plan to destroy Líu Bāng's forces, he grew worried for Zhāng Liáng's safety.

CHINESE SAYINGS BOOK 2
EPISODE 23

05:43 | In a desperate attempt to reconcile the two sides of Chǔ and Hàn, Xiàng Bó leapt on his horse and rushed overnight to Líu Bāng's camp. Once there he gave them the lowdown on what was about to happen and he begged Zhāng Liáng to escape with him.

05:57 | In response to these pleas, Zhāng Liáng said, "It would be disloyal of me to abandon Líu Bāng now." He at once entered Líu Bāng's tent and informed him of Xiàng Yǔ's impending attack.

06:09 | Alarmed, Líu Bāng exclaimed, "What shall we do?"

06:13 | Zhāng Liáng replied, "My lord, who advised you to take over Xiányáng without Xiàng Yǔ in this manner?"

06:20 | Líu Bāng said regretfully, "A petty advisor told me: 'Take over Xiányáng, and from there you will be able to take over all the Qín lands!' So I took his word for it."

06:32 | Zhāng Liáng said, "Well, do you think you will be able to hold off Xiàng Yǔ with your current forces?"

06:37 | Líu Bāng answered, "My army is no match for his!"

06:42 | Zhāng Liáng replied, "My lord, I ask you to give me leave to tell my friend Xiàng Bó that you had no motive of challenging Xiàng Yǔ by entering Xiányáng."

06:52 | Líu Bāng said, "I didn't know you were on friendly terms with Xiàng Bó. Bring him in this minute, and I will receive him as I would receive my own elder brother!"

CHINESE SAYINGS BOOK 2
EPISODE 23

07:00 | When Xiàng Bó came in to meet Líu Bāng, Líu Bāng welcomed him with his best wine, and even drew up a marriage contract between two of their children. Then, he said, "When I entered Xiányáng, I dared not do much without receiving orders from my superior, Xiàng Yǔ. All I did was to take a census of the capital's population, and secure the granaries. Then I told my troops to settle down and await Xiàng Yǔ's arrival. Meanwhile, my army has been guarding the region from thieves and bandits, and we have been looking for Xiàng Yǔ day and night! I have had no thought of rebelling against him, and I hope you will tell him so at once!"

07:37 | Xiàng Bó promised he would, and told Líu Bāng: "You must come as early as you possibly can tomorrow, and inform Xiàng Yǔ so yourself!"

07:46 | Líu Bāng gave his word, and Xiàng Bó leapt back onto his horse and rode overnight back to Xiàng Yǔ's camp, fifty kilometers away to the east, where he told Xiàng Yǔ what Líu Bāng had said, and added: "Out of all the rebels, the Duke of Pèi has made the first foray into the region of Guānzhōng. If it weren't for his efforts, your own forces could hardly have entered this crucial area! What thanks would it be for his bravery if you crushed his army? Instead, you should receive him kindly."

08:16 | Xiàng Yǔ, who was quick to anger but quick to forgive, immediately agreed to Xiàng Bó's word. Thus, when Líu Bāng rode into Xiàng Yǔ's camp at Hóngmén, he found a friendly welcome awaiting him. Líu Bāng explained to Xiàng Yǔ: "My lord, your humble servant joined forces

162

CHINESE SAYINGS BOOK 2
EPISODE 23

with you to rebel against the Qin. You won the region north of the river, and I the region south of the river. By a trick of fate and through no scheme of my own, I was the first to enter the capital at Xiányáng, but now that I have reunited with you, I hope you will not believe the evil rumors spread about my intentions in entering the capital without you."

08:56   Xiàng Yǔ replied, "It was a petty spy who brought me the message that you had delusions of grandeur, or I would never even have considered acting violently against you." Then, he ordered a feast to be prepared in honour of Líu Bāng. The principal guests at this feast were Xiàng Yǔ himself, his advisors Xiàng Bó and Fàn Zēng, and Líu Bāng and his advisor, Zhāng Liáng.

09:22   Fàn Zēng, Xiàng Yǔ's advisor who had originally pushed for military action against Líu Bāng, made several signs to Xiàng Yǔ over the course of the banquet, signaling him to have Líu Bāng assassinated now that he was finally in his grasp. But Xiàng Yǔ pretended to see nothing.

09:40   Desperate, Fàn Zēng left the room and went to speak to Xiàng Zhuāng. He said to him: "Lord Xiàng has mistakenly decided to forgive Líu Bāng and show mercy. The work of assassinating him now falls on you. This is what you need to do. Enter the banquet hall on the pretext of offering wine to Lord Xiàng, and when you have done this, offer to perform a sword-dance for the guests at the feast. In the course of this dance, as soon as you get the opportunity, you take that sword and plunge it into Líu Bāng. If we don't get rid of him now when we have the chance, he will surely come to power, and we will all become his captives in the course of time!"

10:19 Xiàng Zhuāng did as Fàn Zēng suggested, entering to make his toasts to his leader. After these were complete, he said, "This is not much like a real feast; there is no entertainment at all. What if I were to perform a sword-dance for you and your honoured guests?"

10:34 Xiàng Yǔ agreed, and Xiàng Zhuāng unsheathed his sword. Suspecting mischief, Xiàng Bó unsheathed his own sword, and joined Xiàng Zhuāng in performing a sword-dance. He had an idea what Xiàng Zhuāng was up to and made sure to be positioned in such a way that whenever Xiàng Zhuāng's blade got too close to Liu Bang, he would make sure to catch it with his own blade and to shield Líu Bāng's body with his own.

11:01 Seeing that the situation was desperate and that the Duke of Pèi's life was in danger, Zhāng Liáng made excuses and went outside to speak to another of Líu Bāng's advisors, Fán Kuài 樊哙. Fán Kuài hurriedly asked, "How are things inside the tent?"

11:17 Zhāng Liáng replied, "Desperate indeed! Xiàng Zhuāng is right in the middle of performing a sword-dance, but his weapon often comes too close to the Duke of Pèi for my liking."

11:29 Fán Kuài replied: "There isn't a moment to lose! I will live and die with the Duke of Pèi!"

CHINESE SAYINGS BOOK 2
EPISODE 23

11:35 | Saying this, he made to go inside the banquet tent, fully armed. Xiàng Yǔ's guard tried to bar his entry, but he pushed them aside with his sword and shield, and burst into the tent panting and glaring at Xiàng Yǔ, all his hair standing on end.

11:51 | Xiàng Yǔ's hand went to the hilt of his sword and he cried, "Who is this intruder?"

11:56 | Zhāng Liáng quickly explained, "This is one of the Duke of Peì's advisors, Fán Kuài."

12:02 | "What a brave-looking warrior!" said Xiàng Yǔ, his fears assuaged. "Give him wine!"

12:08 | Fán Kuài drank down the decanter of wine in one gulp. Impressed, Xiàng Yǔ ordered, "Give him some meat!"

12:16 | A whole leg of pork, not yet cooked fully through, was laid in front of Fán Kuài. Using his shield as a plate, Fán Kuài, without any fear of contracting trichinosis, made quick work of the meat with the aid of his sword.

12:31 | "Wahhh! A brave warrior indeed!" exclaimed Xiàng Yǔ. "Can you handle another drink?"

12:36 | "A drink?" replied Fán Kuài. "I am not afraid of death, to say nothing of another drink! I came to speak to you of the Qin Emperor, who had the heart of a wolf or a tiger, cruel enough to massacre people at his slightest whim. There were not enough people in all the land to satisfy his murderous will. Thus, all under Heaven rebelled

CHINESE SAYINGS BOOK 2
EPISODE 23

against him. When we set off on our mission against the Qín, we were told, 'He who first enters Xiányáng will surely become the new lord of all under Heaven.' Thus, when the Duke of Pèi captured Xiányáng, in deference to your authority, he refused to lay a finger on it except to shut off the palaces and granaries, and to guard Xiányáng's passes against bandits and thieves. Now, his armies have retreated to Bàshàng (霸上) to await your arrival in Xiányáng. All this he has done, and you have not rewarded him with lands or titles, but have instead chosen to believe the word of petty thieves and spies. Indeed, you were on the point of siccing your armies on him! This is exactly the sort of behaviour that brought about the Qín Emperor's downfall. He who wishes to be China's new Emperor, should never resort to it!"

13:47   Xiàng Yǔ had no reply to this; he ordered Fán Kuài to sit. Fán Kuài accordingly sat by Zhāng Liáng. But not long after this, Líu Bāng excused himself to go to the relieve his bladder, whereupon Fán Kuài followed him outside the tent and begged him to escape at once from Xiàng Yǔ's camp, as they all feared for his life.

14:09   After the two men had talked for a time, Xiàng Yǔ sent a messenger to summon them back to the feast. Líu Bāng said, "How can I escape at once without taking my leave of Xiàng Yǔ?"

14:21   Fán Kuài said, "The matter at hand is too important for dilly-dallying, and in the pursuit of larger ends, small transgressions are excusable. Right now, they are the cleaver and chopping board, and we are morsels of meat

CHINESE SAYINGS BOOK 2
EPISODE 23

and fish! How can you think of matters of etiquette?"

14:38 Líu Bāng saw that Fán Kuài was right and the two men decided to flee Hóngmén on horseback without further ado, leaving behind their carriages and entourage. Líu Bāng asked Zhāng Liáng to stay and soften his sudden absence with the gift of a pair of fine jades: "My camp and Xiàng Yǔ's are only forty li apart. Wait till I have ridden halfway there, and then make my excuses!"

15:03 Zhāng Liáng waited for the time it took for a horse to gallop twenty lǐ 里 or about three miles, and then he reentered the banquet tent to tell Xiàng Yǔ that Líu Bāng had begged him to take leave of Xiàng Yǔ on his behalf, since Líu Bāng could not handle his drink. Xiàng Yǔ accepted these excuses, but his advisor Fàn Zēng was furious.

15:23 "I curse the day I came into Xiàng Yǔ's employ! The man is truly not a worthy commander!" he ranted. "How could he be so blind as to let Líu Bāng escape from under his very eye? The man who takes all under Heaven from Xiàng Yǔ will be Líu Bāng! From this day on, I am no better than Líu Bāng's captive!"

15:43 Well, you know the rest. In this act carried out at Hóngmén, Swan Goose Gate, the civil war remembered as the Chǔ Hàn Xiāngzhèng, the Chu Han Contention, pitted the forces of Xiàng Yǔ against Liú Bāng. And these two fought it out over a period of years lasting from 206 to 202 BC. And just as was predicted by Xiàng Yǔ's advisers, indeed Liu Bang emerged victorious, crushing

CHINESE SAYINGS BOOK 2
EPISODE 23

Xiàng Yǔ's army at Gàixià in northern Ānhuī province. This is where Xiàng Yǔ fell to Liu Bang and committed suicide. And the year 202 BC became a milestone in Chinese history. For this was the year the Hàn Dynasty was established.

16:27 So, Xiàng Zhuāng wǔjiàn, yìzài Pèi Gōng. Xiàng Zhuāng performs a sword dance with the intention to harm the Duke of Pèi.

16:36 And from this famous story from ancient times, this chengyu has come to mean someone is acting with a hidden motive. If you see yourself getting set up for a fall or someone appears to be helping you but they're actually plotting your demise, you can say those guys are Xiàng Zhuāng wǔjiàn, yìzài Pèi Gōng.

16:58 These eight syllables can be used metaphorically to describe any deceptive or hidden agenda behind someone's actions or words. It implies that while someone may appear friendly and benign, their true intentions are to do you harm. When you see your friend walking into a possible trap, you can remind them Xiàng Zhuāng wǔjiàn, yìzài Pèi Gōng. And if they're familiar with the story behind this great chengyu, they'll know to stay vigilant and not be fooled by appearances.

17:27 So there you have it. Xiàng Zhuāng wǔjiàn, yìzài Pèi Gōng Xiàng Zhuāng doing that sword dance, aiming to do irreparable harm to the Duke of Pèi. And had he succeeded we may never have had a Hàn Dynasty. Perhaps it would have been the Chǔ Dynasty instead.

CHINESE SAYINGS BOOK 2
EPISODE 23

17:46 | There was a movie made about this Hóngmén Yàn, this Banquet at Hóngmén, in 2011. The English title was White Vengeance. I'll put a link at the show notes if you want to check it out....I found it on YouTube.

17:59 | Until the next time, this here's Laszlo Montgomery thanking you for listening and welcoming you to come back again next time for another illuminating episode of the Chinese Sayings Podcast.

 Chinese Sayings Book 2
Episode 24

LOOKS CAN BE DECEIVING

华而不实—Huá Ér Bù Shí

TRANSCRIPT

00:00 Greetings everyone, all you fans of Chinese Sayings, Laszlo Montgomery here with one more chengyu for your ever-expanding collezione. And for the sixth offering in this 8th season of the show that forever remains true to its name, Emma and I came up with a good one for you.

00:20 And not just good, but useful too. Huá Ér Bù Shí. This one doesn't take long to tell and I'll have you on your way in no time at all. Let's break down the four characters and get right to the story.

00:33 Huá Ér Bù Shí. What can that mean?

00:36 Huá, besides being an abbreviation for China, usually means 'glory.' But in this particular case, Huá is standing in for the character Huā which means flower.

00:49 Ér is a conjunction which means but, yet, or on the other hand.

CHINESE SAYINGS BOOK 2
EPISODE 24

00:54	And Bù means no or not.
00:59	And Shí, as a noun, in the second tone means fruit, but more commonly it means reality or fact. As an adjective shí can also mean true or real. In this chéngyǔ it means fruit, and I'll explain why in a bit.
01:13	And for the second time this season, and at least the fourth or fifth time in the history of this show that first surfaced back in 2016, the good old days, we're taking the Chronicles of Zuǒ off the shelf to get the backstory behind this one. In the chapter Wén Gōng Wǔnián 文公五年, The Fifth Year of Duke Wén, we get Huá Ér Bù Shí.
01:5	And the Zuǒ Zhuàn being Zuǒ Qiūmíng's annotations to the Spring and Autumn Annals, this story takes place around then, sometime 630-620 BC. This was the time of Dukes Wén of Jìn featured earlier this Season in Tui Bi San She, as well as Duke Mù of Qín when he was in his prime. Heady years in those decades of the Eastern Zhou.
02:00	Our main character is someone of no particular consequence. His name was Yáng Chǔfù 阳处父. He was a state minister of Jìn 晋.
02:09	So it's around this time that the well-intentioned Zhou Dynasty founded in 1046 BC by Kings Wén and Wǔ with a little help from the Duke of Zhou, started to break down. The 7th century BC saw China, Northern China that is, engulfed in territorial disputes with bordering states.

CHINESE SAYINGS BOOK 2
EPISODE 24

02:31 | Besides attacking each other, they also engaged in a robust diplomacy. Jìn was having a particularly challenging time with Chǔ to their south. In an effort to resume friendly relations, Duke Wén of Jìn sent his minister Yáng Chǔfù on a diplomatic mission to the state of Chǔ.

02:51 | So he went down to Chǔ, passed on the messages from his king and promptly returned to Jìn. On his way from Chǔ, Yáng Chǔfù passed the small town of Níngyì 宁邑, today just north of Zhèngzhōu, where he was obliged to stop for the night at a local inn owned by a man surnamed Yíng. Same surname as the Qín royal family.

03:13 | Innkeeper Yíng was struck by Yáng Chǔfù's impressive looks and his way with words and how he carried himself. This simple innkeeper was wowed by Yáng's dignified appearance and hung on Yáng Chǔfù's every word, listening to him late into the night. On and on Yáng Chǔfù went about all his good deeds, worldly knowledge and long list of accomplishments. And Innkeeper Yíng could hardly believe that such a great man was staying at his humble establishment.

03:47 | So impressed was Innkeeper Yíng, in fact, he took his wife aside and said to her: "I have always wanted to leave this small town and offer my services to a great and virtuous man. In my line of business, I have seen many people come and go, but I have never met a man whom I felt I could safely follow. Today Yáng Chǔfù has come to our town and is staying at our inn. This must be a sign from heaven! He must be the man I was meant to follow."

04:16 | After making his wishes known to Yáng Chǔfù, Innkeeper Yíng was accepted as part of Yáng Chǔfù's retinue. In high spirits, Innkeeper Yíng tidied up his business affairs, said goodbye to his wife, and embarked on the journey back to Jìn with Yáng Chǔfù.

04:36 | Imagine his wife's surprise when, not long after his departure from their small town, her husband suddenly appeared back at the inn! She could not help remarking: You spoke so highly of his character and talent! And you left your business and family well provided for, so you need not have returned on our account. Why then have you come back to Níngyì?"

04:59 | Innkeeper Yíng sighed. "We had not even departed the borders of Níngyì before I realized that Yáng Chǔfù was not what he seemed on first glance. As I listened to him boasting about the same great deeds over and over again, and observed his treatment of others more closely, I realized that he was nothing but a foolish man, all dressed up in those fine garments, with an impulsive temper and an inflated opinion of himself.

05:27 | "All his good looks and tall tales are just for show. He is like a branch that blossoms but does not bear fruit. I was afraid that if I continued as part of his retinue, not only would I not get the education necessary to become a virtuous and educated man myself, but I might in fact get caught up in something I'd regret. So I cut my losses and came back home."

CHINESE SAYINGS BOOK 2
EPISODE 24

05:51 So Yáng Chǔfù with all his self-importance and dignitas that he wrapped himself up in, he sure fooled this innkeeper. Poor old Mr. Yíng thought that this chance encounter with someone the likes of Yáng Chǔfù was going to lead to some kind of opportunity or a chance to rise up to a higher station in life.

06:12 And when his chance came, he took it and then he found out, boy did he ever judge this book by its cover. This guy turned out to be Huá Ér Bù Shí, like a tree that flowers but doesn't bear fruit. Innkeeper Yíng misjudged this man's character.

06:29 Hey, we all know, looks can be deceiving and they sure were in this case. Innkeeper Yíng learned the hard way. When he realized his benefactor was huá, all flowery and looking good on the outside. Ér Bù Shí but, with no real substance. Worse than an empty suit. So Innkeeper Yíng, he turned on his heels and got back to where he once belonged.

06:53 And when his wife wanted an explanation, all Mr. Ying really had to say were those four syllables. He didn't even need a rejoinder. Huá ér bù shí. Nuff said.

07:05 Okay, thanks to Zuǒ Qiūmíng one more time for giving us this one.

07:10 So that's gonna be all she wrote for this time. Remember, when it comes to people, sometimes you can never tell. Huá ér bù shí. Okay, this is Laszlo Montgomery signing off from Los Angeles, California. Thanks for listening

CHINESE SAYINGS BOOK 2
EPISODE 24

and I cordially invite you all to come back next time for another exciting episode of the Chinese Sayings Podcast.

Chinese Sayings Book 2
Episode 25

HELP!

涸辙之鲋—Hé Zhé Zhī Fù

TRANSCRIPT

00:00 | Greetings once again all lovers of Chinese Sayings. Laszlo Montgomery here with another good chéngyǔ. This one's another short one. But it comes from Zhuāngzǐ which more than makes up for the brevity. He's been featured in more than a couple episodes going back to Season 1.

00:17 | Today we look at the story behind Hé Zhé Zhī Fù 涸辙之鲋. This one is kind of related to Fǔ Dǐ Yóu Yú 釜底游鱼 from Season 4 Episode 10. I'll explain later.

00:28 | So, let's run through the four characters Hé Zhé Zhī Fù.

00:32 | Hé means dried or to dry up.

00:36 | And a Zhé is a kind of rut that is created by tracks made by wheels or carts or other vehicles that ply the roads.

00:45 | And a Zhī once again a character that's used between an attribute and the word it modifies.

177

CHINESE SAYINGS BOOK 2
EPISODE 25

00:53 | And the word it's modifying here is Fù which means a carp.

00:57 | Literal meaning: A Dry Rut Carp.

01:01 | Not that revealing of a clue as to what these four characters mean. But let's find out, shall we?

01:08 | As I said, this four-letter Chinese Saying, we have everyone's favorite, Zhuāngzǐ, to thank. This chéngyǔ was lifted from the Outer Chapters of his eponymous work. If you all recall the Inner Chapters of the Zhuangzi were allegedly written by the man himself. The Outer Chapters, maybe, maybe not.

01:30 | And the gùshi 故事, the story behind this one, it goes like this. Like a lot of brilliant and witty scholars and philosophers of his age, 4th century BC, Zhuāngzǐ was usually focused on his studies and he often neglected his household chores and familial responsibilities. And as a result, he and his family lived in a constant state of stress, poverty, barely keeping their heads above water.

02:00 | One day, Zhuāngzǐ found that, once again, he had nothing to put in his cooking pot. His family was in dire straits and with no income to buy even the barest necessities of life. The great and celebrated Zhuāngzǐ was left with no other recourse but to go cap in hand to a famously wealthy man in his region to borrow some grain.

CHINESE SAYINGS BOOK 2
EPISODE 25

02:25 | Now, this wealthy man was very miserly. He still had the first string of copper cash he ever earned. But when the usually high-and-mighty, not to mention the famous Zhuāngzǐ came to ask for grain at his doorstep, he saw an opportunity too good to pass up.

02:45 | When Zhuāngzǐ knocked on the man's door, he was shown in. After the initial pleasantries Zhuāngzǐ stated the purpose for this visit. The man, all smiles, said to Zhuāngzǐ, "Why, of course I'll lend you some grain! But I can't do it right now. I hope you can wait till after I've collected rents from all the tenants on my land. This might take some time but you have my word, I'll send over a good three hundred jīn of grain to your place. That's more than you could ever want! How about that?"

03:19 | Three hundred jin of grain. That was a few hundred pounds. But Zhuāngzǐ at once saw through the man's soft rejection. It would have been nothing for this old greedy miser to help Zhuāngzǐ and his family out with a little bit of grain. There was no need for him to send over three hundred pounds. They just needed to get by until Zhuāngzǐ was able to earn a bit of cash.

03:43 | Zhuāngzǐ angrily replied, "You know something, I had to walk for many miles to reach your house. Yesterday, on my journey, I heard a small voice crying, 'Help! Help!' I turned around immediately to look for the source of the voice, and saw this little carp lying, half-dead, in a rut left by a cart-wheel. The rut had barely any water left in it from the last rain, and the little fish could barely breathe.

CHINESE SAYINGS BOOK 2
EPISODE 25

04:12 | "So I drew closer to the carp and asked, 'Was it you asking for help? What seems to be the problem?' The carp saw me approaching and began to twitch with joy. 'Sir, I once lived happily in the Eastern Sea, but have now unfortunately fallen into this dry rut! Please, the water is fast evaporating and I am about to suffocate to death! I beg of you to pour merely half a jug of water on me!'"

04:39 | Here, Zhuāngzǐ paused. The wealthy man, listening to the story, said impatiently, "Well, what happened next? Did you agree to save the carp?" Zhuāngzǐ replied coldly, "I said to the carp, 'Of course I'll save you from suffocating. I'm on my way South right now, and when I get to the South, I'll make a special request to the kings of both Wú 吴 and Yuè 越, and ask them to divert the flood of the southern rivers to this very spot and when the waters come rushing in, you'll be saved. How about that? Would that be okay?"

05:11 | How did the carp reply, asked the old miser. Zhuāngzǐ looked at the old man and said, "The carp was furious to hear my reply. Leaping around in anger, it said to me, 'I asked you for half a jug of water, not the flood of the rivers of the South! If that's how you're planning to save my life, then you might as well look for me tomorrow at the market at one of the dried fish stalls!'"

05:36 | So this poor old Hé Zhé zhī Fù, this Carp in a dry rut with barely enough water to let him breathe, he became a metaphor for anyone who's on their last legs and on the cusp of perishing or going down for the count.

CHINESE SAYINGS BOOK 2
EPISODE 25

05:53 | Anyone in this kind of a desperate situation can be called a Hé Zhé zhī Fù. A carp in a dry rut. So if you ever find yourself in a similar situation, think of the poor old carp.

06:07 | I mentioned at the outset this chéngyǔ is a cousin to Fǔ Dǐ Yóu Yú 釜底游魚 featured in Season 4. Some of you may recall the bandit leader Zhāng Yīng lamenting that due to the wickedness of the times he and his men lived like a fish, swimming at the bottom of a cooking pot, desperate for a few last gasps of air.

06:27 | Yeah, no shortage of Chinese Sayings that describe being in desperate straits. And now you have one more for your ever expanding collezione. Hé Zhé zhī Fù, the carp in the dry rut.

06:41 | Okay, thanks everyone for listening. This is Laszlo Montgomery once again beseeching you to join me next time for another episode from this podcast show that has stayed true to its name since 2016, the Chinese Sayings Podcast.

**Chinese Sayings Book 2
Episode 26**

LET'S STICK TOGETHER

物以类聚—Wù Yǐ Lèi Jù

TRANSCRIPT

00:00 Good morning or good evening wherever you may be in this wonderful but troubled world, Laszlo Montgomery here with another fine offering for you from the Chinese Sayings Podcast.

00:12 And for the eighth time this season I have another nice chéngyǔ for you. The meaning behind this one has an equivalent in many different languages, Wù Yǐ Lèi Jù 物以类聚. And like most but not all of these Chinese Sayings introduced in this, well, I guess by now you can also call it a long running family program, it comes to us from the Warring States Period. But before we get the story, let's quickly break it down character by character and see if we can figure out the meaning.

00:41 Wù Yǐ Lèi Jù.

00:44 Wù means a thing, or substance or a creature.

CHINESE SAYINGS BOOK 2
EPISODE 26

00:47 | Yǐ is a preposition that means with, by means of, or according to. It can also mean because of.

00:55 | Lèi means kind, type, class or category or something that is similar.

01:03 | And the fourth character Jù means to assemble, congregate or gather together.

01:09 | Cobble that all together and we get: thing according to type assemble.

01:15 | Some of you can make a calculated guess about what this means. But just in case, lend me your ear and I'll tell you the story and try not to sing out of key. Even when the four characters give away the meaning, it's still good to hear the backstory so that these four characters come really come alive.

01:34 | This is an old chengyu that first appeared as one of the principles in the Yì Jīng 易经, The Book of Changes. You can also find it as an adage taken from the Strategies of the Warring States, the Zhànguó Cè that was compiled during the Western Hàn dynasty.

01:50 | And our story for today comes specifically from a chapter in the Strategies of the Warring States called The Strategies of Qí 齐策, the Qí Cè.

01:59 | In this one, we welcome back to the CSP King Wēi of Qí 齐威王, Qí Wēi Wáng, one of the great and consequential 4th century BC rulers of China. He reigned in Qí from

184

CHINESE SAYINGS BOOK 2
EPISODE 26

356 to 320 BC and was the first ruler of Qí to call himself a king rather than a duke.

02:19 When this duke who became a king ascended to the throne, the Kingdom left to him by his father Tián Qí Huán Gōng 田齐桓公, it was still recovering from prodigious amounts of internal turmoil. And this son who we remember as King Wēi of Qí, before he became this great and powerful ruler, initially showed no signs of taking his position seriously.

02:42 Instead of mopping up from his father's rule by reorganizing the Qí court and strengthening the Qí borders, the future King Wēi let his newfound power and wealth go to his head, frittering away his time on expensive wines and pleasures of the flesh.

02:59 But fortunately he had in his employ a very talented and capable minister named Chúnyú Kūn 淳于髡. Chúnyú Kūn, besides being a minister to the king, was also a philosopher and a personal friend of Mèngzǐ, I might add. He was also known as one of the great witty intellectuals of his day and has plenty of stories attributed to him, including this one.

03:23 He was one of those guys who, like a court jester perhaps, was able to speak truths to the king that no one else would dare utter. And he was especially famous for the witty, indirect phrases he used to make the king see reason.

03:41 King Wēi of Qí kept up a busy regimen of hanging out and wasting time while his kingdom started to degrade.

CHINESE SAYINGS BOOK 2
EPISODE 26

This went on for three years, during which time Qí's neighbors, seeing Qí's internal weakness, began harrying its borders. The Qí court ministers were tearing their hair out at this situation, but none of them dared to bring up the problem directly to the king until Chúnyú Kūn came up with a clever way to put it to him nicely.

04:10 He went to King Wēi one day and said, "Your Majesty, I have heard that there is a large bird in the Qí kingdom, who makes its nest in the eaves of this very palace. This bird is so lazy that for three years it has neither flown nor crowed. Can you tell me why this might be?"

04:30 King Wēi stopped short at this indirect yet brave rebuke of his obvious failures to rule properly. After considering for some time, he made his reply in the same vein: "This bird has not flown for three years, but once it flies, it will reach the very heavens. This bird has also not crowed for three years, but when you hear its first crow it will astonish all who hear it."

05:00 Now, I don't mean to interrupt this program or anything, but this very reply by King Wēi also became a famous chéngyǔ. You see, this retort to Chúnyú Kūn's remark about the bird that didn't do diddly squat for three years went like this: Bù fēi zéyǐ, yī fēi chōngtiān; bù míng zéyǐ, yīmíng jīngrén 不飞则已，一飞冲天;不鸣则已，一鸣惊人.

05:23 This reply is the source of the well-known chengyu, Yī Míng Jīng Rén 一鸣惊人 to describe unexpected brilliance from, usually an unknown person. To amaze the world

CHINESE SAYINGS BOOK 2
EPISODE 26

with a single brilliant feat and becoming an overnight sensation. Someone who takes the world by storm with a single deed.

05:42 True to his words, King Wēi immediately began to shape up and give the kingdom his full attention. He tended to the affairs of his kingdom. He proved himself to be a diligent and intelligent king who soon managed to strengthen and reinforce his Qí kingdom. He also recognized Chúnyú Kūn's true value as an advisor, since Chúnyú Kūn was the only one who had been brave enough to admonish him.

06:09 In 349 B.C., down in the present day lands of Húběi and Húnán, King Xuān of Chǔ sent soldiers to invade Qí. With Chúnyú Kūn's help, King Wēi of Qí managed to form an alliance with the Marquess of Zhào, Sù Hóu 肃侯. And together Qí and Zhào were able to beat back the Chǔ invasion.

06:32 In the wake of this victory, King Wēi held a large celebratory banquet, which was so excessive that it resembled the old bacchanals he used to hold during his profligate days. At this banquet, he challenged his favorite minister Chúnyú Kūn to a drinking game.

06:50 Chúnyú Kūn responded thus: Jiǔjí zéluàn, lèjí shēngbēi 酒极则乱, 乐极生悲 "Drinking to excess leads to chaos, just as unrestrained joy leads to sorrow." Again, Chúnyú Kūn's words had the effect of sobering up King Wēi, who realized the inherent dangers in the excessiveness of the celebrations he was holding.

07:19 After King Wēi died, his son ascended to the throne as King Xuān in 320 BC. One of King Xuān's first acts was to order all the current court ministers to recommend new talent to him who could be recruited to aid in governing the kingdom. Believe it or not on that very day King Xuān's edict was publicized, Chúnyú Kūn recommended not one, not two, but seven talented men to the king.

07:47 When King Xuān interviewed each of these men, he found that, to a man, they were all intelligent, strategically-minded, and virtuous, and suitable for employment at his royal court. He was delighted, but also curious about how Chúnyú Kūn was able to run across seven men of such high calibre at the drop of a hat.

08:08 Thus, King Xuān summoned Chúnyú Kūn, and said, "Minister, I am curious about your methods of finding virtuous men. The sages have said that a man of true virtue is not to be found for a thousand lǐ. The sages have also said that a man of true virtue does not appear more than once every hundred generations. Yet you have at once recommended to me seven virtuous men. By this reckoning, the sages must be wrong, and men of virtue seem to grow as thickly as weeds on the ground."

08:42 And here is where we finally get to the punchline. Chúnyú Kūn smiled in response. "Your Majesty, it is not that men of virtue are naturally to be found so easily. Rather, just as natural objects congregate with others of the same species, we humans too are attracted to others of a similar character. You have observed birds of the

CHINESE SAYINGS BOOK 2
EPISODE 26

---

same kind flying together and roosting together, and you have no doubt also observed beasts of the same species herding together and traveling together. And surely you see certain grasses and herbs do not grow at all in lowlands and marshes, but when you go to seek them in the mountains, you'll find them by the cartload. Thus you can see that everything in nature is attracted to other things that are of a similar nature.

09:32 "Now, I choose to spend my time only with virtuous men, and I make it a point to only befriend men of noble character and prodigious talent. Thus, sourcing men of talent for me is as easy as drawing water from a river or coaxing fire from a flint stone. And I know far more talented and virtuous men than just the seven I have recommended to you today, and I'll continue to recommend them to you in the future."

09:57 And so this Chinese Saying, Wù Yǐ Lèi Jù, is the Chinese version of our English idiom, "birds of a feather flock together."

10:06 And as I said at the outset, in other places where different languages are spoken they also have their own idioms to describe how living things tend to group together according to their similarities in nature. In Deutschland they might say Gleich und Gleich gesellt sich gern. In La France they say Qui se ressemble s'assemble. And two and a half hours south from where I'm recording this they might say Dios los cría y el viento los amontona.

10:35	But however you wants to say it, it all means Wù Yǐ Lèi Jù. We and all natural living things down to the krill in the oceans, we all like to stick to our own kind. It's a natural thang. Wù Yǐ Lèi Jù. Even all well-traveled and open-minded folks of all kinds, well, they might be amenable to any kind of new culture but at the end of the day we all be Wù Yǐ Lèi Jù.
11:00	And so, signing off the the eighth time already in this eighth season, this is Laszlo Montgomery. My deepest thanks if you made it this far. Do consider coming back again next time for another exciting episode of the Chinese Sayings Podcast.

Chinese Sayings Book 2
Episode 27

WHY CAN'T WE LIVE TOGETHER?

势不两立—Shì Bù Liǎng Lì

TRANSCRIPT

00:00 Welcome back ladies and gentlemans, Laszlo Montgomery with you again. If you're looking for the Chinese Sayings Podcast, you're tuned to the right station.

00:11 As you can see, there's been a slight fall off in the number of episodes that are usually produced from this long-running family program. You know, the Hollywood writers' strike and all. But we're back today with one that is all too familiar with us as we painfully wend our way through this third decade of the 21st century.

00:32 This time we look at the Chinese saying Shì Bù Liǎng Lì. All fans of the Three Kingdoms know this one, I'm sure. But before I get right on it, let's look at the four characters of this chéngyǔ.

00:46 Shì Bù Liǎng Lì. Four syllables as usual, standard equipment for most Chinese sayings.

CHINESE SAYINGS BOOK 2
EPISODE 27

00:53 Shì means power, force, or influence. And like most Chinese characters it can mean a whole lot else.

01:02 And Bù means no or not or won't.

01:06 Liǎng means the number two when used before Chinese counter words. Or it can also mean both or either when talking about two opposing sides...which is the case in our story today.

01:18 And lastly the character Lì means to stand.

01:23 Power not a couple stand. Hard to tell, but I smell a war or a battle somewhere contained within those four words. So let's get to the story. In the Zhànguó Cè, the Strategies of the Warring States, one of the great reservoirs of Chinese Sayings, this chéngyǔ first appears.

01:44 This ancient classic text that gave us so much insight into the Warring States Period, originally referred to the kingdoms of Qín and Chǔ, two rivals whose enmity at times, gave us the phrase, Fán tiānxià jiāngguó, fēi Qín yě Chǔ, fēi Chǔ ér Qín, liǎngguó jiāozhēng, qí shì bù liǎng lì. 凡天下彊国，非秦而楚，非楚而秦，两国交争，其势不两立 which essentially means "When Chǔ is strong, Qín is weak; when Qín is strong, Chǔ is weak. The two cannot co-exist."

02:20 There were seven Warring States who battled it out from roughly 476 to 221 BC. And true to those words, the kingdom of Chǔ was defeated in 223 BC by Qín, led by their king, Yíng Zhèng who went on to found the Qín

CHINESE SAYINGS BOOK 2
EPISODE 27

Dynasty in 221 BC and gain immortality as the First emperor of a unified China, Qín Shǐhuáng.

02:46 So Shì Bù Liǎng Lì can refer to the inability of the two great powers of Qín and Chǔ not being able to co-exist. However, this Chinese saying, Shì Bù Liǎng Lì, is perhaps more famously remembered for its inclusion in the Records of the Three Kingdoms, the Sān Guó Zhì. It comes specifically from the chapter Zhōu Yú Zhuàn 周瑜传, the Biography of Zhōu Yú. And from this story about the hero Zhōu Yú, this chéngyǔ is best remembered.

03:20 The Records of the Three Kingdoms was the essential source that Míng Dynasty author Luó Guànzhōng used to produce his masterwork, the Romance of the Three Kingdoms. One of the great Chinese classic novels of all time.

03:36 So, let's set it up. On the eve of the epic Battle of Red Cliffs in 208 A.D., Sūn Quán, general and future Emperor of Eastern Wu, one of the Three Kingdoms of that age, found himself having to make a crucial decision. Sūn Quán and his Wú army of 30,000 troops were encamped not too far from Red Cliffs, along the Yangzi River in today's Hubei province. He knew that the opposing general, Cáo Cāo of Wèi, another of the Three Kingdoms, was preparing for an attack south of the Yangzi. Cáo Cāo had moreover sent a rather threatening letter to Sūn Quán, saying that he had 800,000 troops who could easily destroy Sūn Quán's 30,000. And in his letter Cáo Cāo promised Sūn Quán leniency if he would surrender before engaging in battle.

04:35	In the wake of Cáo Cāo's letter to Sūn Quán, the third general and future leader of Shǔ, Líu Bèi, also sent an emissary to Sūn Quán. Líu Bèi asked Sūn Quán to consider joining forces with him to defeat Cáo Cāo.
04:50	But Sūn Quán knew very well that Líu Bèi had even fewer resources than himself. Líu Bèi's army numbered only 10,000 soldiers. Considering this offer by Liú Bèi to be inconsequential. Sūn Quán chose to go it alone and to go up against Cáo Cāo. Choosing this course, Sūn Quán would have to bear the brunt of Cáo Cāo's forces.
05:8	Sūn Quán called a council of war with his most trusted advisors. Opinions were divided. Some considered accepting Cáo Cāo's offer of leniency the safest course of action.
05:32	But one of Sūn Quán's most trusted advisors, Zhōu Yú, stood up and said: "Our enemies are not as strong as you think; nor as you fear, are our own soldiers so weak. Cáo Cāo has not managed to fully pacify Northern China. He also has undefeated enemies in the Shǎnxī region that will no doubt come back to plague him one day. What's more, in coming south to attack us, Cáo Cāo has had to rely on naval forces and not his cavalry. Now, we are soldiers of Wú from the Jiāngnán region, and we are experts in river battles and watery terrain. Cáo Cāo's forces are from the Central Plains region of the north and know almost nothing about fighting on water. Besides, it is winter, and leading a massive force of soldiers from the Central Plains to the Yangzi River means that not only will they be hard pressed to find

CHINESE SAYINGS BOOK 2
EPISODE 27

fodder for their cavalry, but they will also undoubtedly fall ill in this unfamiliar Yangzi river climate. Any good general would have thought twice about leading his soldiers into battle under such conditions, but Cáo Cāo wants to do it nonetheless."

06:49 Zhōu Yú sincerely told Sūn Quán, "If you consider the situation from this perspective, there is really no better time than now to win a decisive victory against Cáo Cāo. I myself promise that, if you give me command of your 30,000 troops and allow me to lead them into battle, I will defeat Cáo Cāo's Wèi army."

07:12 To this, Sūn Quán replied, "That old thief Cáo Cāo has been concerning me for some time with his blatant ambition to get rid of the Han dynasty emperor and install himself in his place. The only reason he hasn't done this yet is because he fears four people: Yuán Shào (袁绍), Yuán Shù (袁术), Líu Biǎo, and me. Now with the other three having long been defeated by Cáo Cāo, that leaves me as the only one left standing in his way."

07:44 And here Sūn Quán uttered the immortal words of the chengyu featured in this episode. Here he declared to Zhōu Yú, Cáo Cāo and I cannot exist peacefully in this world at the same time, and your advice exactly suits my wishes. It is as if Heaven sent you to aid me in my decision! Sūn Quán knew, as far as his mortal enemy Cáo Cāo was concerned, it was a case of Shì Bù Liǎng Lì. The two of them could not exist side by side. Only one could be left standing.

08:20	And everyone familiar with the Romance of the Three Kingdoms or sat through the great John Woo's epic film, is aware, because of Zhōu Yú's recommendation, Sūn Quán ultimately decided to join forces with Líu Bèi and together they jointly took on Cáo Cāo.
08:40	Because of Zhōu Yú's ingenious strategies during the Battle of the Red Cliffs, the combined forces of Sūn Quán and Líu Bèi were able to defeat Cáo Cāo's mighty Wèi army and push them back from the regions south of the Yangzi and in so doing, they defused this grave threat to their existence.
09:02	Shì Bù Liǎng Lì. The two forces cannot simultaneously exist. Things be mutually exclusive all around. When two enemies filled with nothing but contempt for each other are fated to live in a single land, peaceful coexistence is simply out of the question. In circumstances like this, Shì Bù Liǎng Lì can be used.
09:27	Whenever the bad blood and tortured history behind two irreconcilable foes is too great, that's where the chengyu Shì Bù Liǎng Lì can be used. Only one can exist, not both. Our last hundred years on our endangered planet has been plagued with neighboring nations filled with animus, antagonism, hatred and hostility for each other. And because of this, their mutual feelings were Shì Bù Liǎng Lì. The land wasn't big enough for the both of them. And we can't even begin to guess how much suffering there has been among the people due to this irreconcilable malignity.

CHINESE SAYINGS BOOK 2
EPISODE 27

10:11 | Shì Bù Liǎng Lì. We know from this story from the later Hàn Dynasty that this line of thinking, that two nations and peoples cannot exist at the same time went back at least to the 3rd century AD.

10:26 | As the late Rodney King once so eloquently said, "Can't we all just get along?"

10:32 | Okay, one more to go for this season. And then that's gonna be it for me for a while. But rest assured, barring the end of civilization on this earth, I'll be back again for a whole new slate of chengyu's in Season 9.

10:46 | Until the next time Mes bons amis partout dans le monde, this is Laszlo Montgomery signing off from Heart Attack and Vine in the city of LA, inviting you to come back again next time for another entertaining episode of the Chinese Sayings Podcast.

Chinese Sayings Book 2
Episode 28

PLEASE ALLOW ME TO INTRODUCE MYSELF

毛遂自荐—Máo Suì Zì Jiàn

TRANSCRIPT

00:00 | Hey everyone, welcome back to the Chinese Sayings Podcast. I thank you all for tuning in and listening.

00:08 | Today we look at a chéngyǔ that I would put in the well-known category. That is to say, it's pretty well-known. Máo Suì Zì Jiàn. This one has a nice backstory and takes place in the Warring States Period, that richest and most fertile time when some of the best and longest lasting chengyu's emerged.

00:29 | And for the sixteenth or seventeenth time already, we're reaching into that veritable goldmine of chengyu's and great stories from ancient China, the Record of the Grand Historian. This one comes from the chapter Píngyuán Jūn Yúqīng Lièzhuàn <史记:平原君虞卿列传>, the Biography of Yúqīng, Lord Píngyuán.

00:51 | This Lord Píngyuán or Píngyuán Jūn, was also called Zhào Shèng 赵胜. He was the younger brother of King Huìwén of Zhào 赵惠文王 and served as chancellor to

199

CHINESE SAYINGS BOOK 2
EPISODE 28

both King Huìwén and his successor, Lord Píngyuán's nephew King Xiàochéng 赵孝成王. From the start of Huìwén to the end of Xiàochéng was 298 to 245 BC.

01:14 Lord Píngyuán lived from 308 to 251 BC. This was during a very consequential time in the history of Zhào and the whole Warring States Period. And we'll get to all of that in the story behind this chéngyǔ: Máo Suì Zìjiàn.

01:31 As far as the four characters that make up this Chinese Saying, Máo Suì, that was a person's name. He was not anyone of particular consequence from greater Chinese history and to be honest, not even from this time. We don't know the dates when he lived. We assume, because the Grand Historian went to the trouble to mention him, that he did once walk this earth.

01:54 And Zìjiàn, this means to recommend yourself, to step up and volunteer.

02:01 So Máo Suì Zìjiàn means Máo Suì volunteers himself.

02:06 Let's dive right into the story. Mid-3rd century BC, we all know it won't be long before Yíng Zhèng, the King of Qín, puts an end to the other six warring states. Pretty much since the mid-4th century BC, Qín State had commenced its Long March to unify China. And under the long-reigning Qín King Zhāoxiāng 秦昭襄王, Qín was proving to be an unstoppable force who put constant stress on the other warring states. Zhāoxiāng was the grandfather to the first emperor, Qín Shǐhuáng

CHINESE SAYINGS BOOK 2
EPISODE 28

02:43 By this time in Chinese history, late Warring States, just before unification in 221 BC, the remaining states knew without forming alliances they'd all be swallowed up by Qín. Zhào's number came up in the year 262 BC when their army clashed with the Qín army led by one of the most victorious generals in world history, Bái Qǐ, at Chángpíng, today's Gāopíng 高平 in Shānxī Province near the Hénán border.

03:15 This battle yielded that old chengyu from season 6 episode 6, Zhǐshàng Tánbīng 纸上谈兵. How can we forget Zhào Kuò? He could defeat any opponent on paper, but when it came to the real thing, he learned right quick about the chasm that often existed between theory and reality.

03:38 In 260 BC, the ever-victorious Qín general Bái Qǐ 白起 annihilated the Zhào army and there are stories that say 450,000 Zhao soldiers perished in this conflict, many of them allegedly buried alive on Bái Qǐ's orders.

03:55 Well, despite this disastrous defeat, Zhào still managed to hang in there for another thirty-eight years until 222 BC when King Yíng Zhèng put them away for good. And after Chángpíng, the Qín army couldn't resist sticking it to Zhào and they continued to attack them. In 259 Qin laid siege to the Zhào capital in present day Hándān 邯郸, right at the southern border of Hebei.

04:21 Unable to break the siege, Zhào King Xiàochéng 赵孝成王, in 257 BC, called in his uncle, Lord Píngyuán and told him unless they could get some help from the kingdom

CHINESE SAYINGS BOOK 2
EPISODE 28

of Chǔ to the south, it was gonna be curtains for Zhào. After discussing the matter, it was agreed that Lord Píngyuán would select twenty capable men among his three thousand ménkè 门客 or followers, to accompany him on this secret mission to Chǔ where he planned to meet with their King Kǎoliè 楚考烈王 and try to enlist his help in sending troops to break this siege Qin had set up around the Zhào capital.

04:59 When Lord Píngyuán was selecting his twenty men, he got as far as nineteen and had some trouble finding that last member of his delegation to Chǔ. As the time passed, one of his hangers on, Máo Suì, stepped forward and volunteered himself to Lord Píngyuán. He said, let me be your twentieth man and help out in this dark hour for Zhào.

05:23 Lord Píngyuán was sort of taken aback and asked, first of all, who are you. I see you serve among my retainers but I don't think I recall ever seeing you before. Máo Suì replied that he had worked in the capital for three years now and had been serving loyally. To which Lord Píngyuán replied frankly, you must not be too terribly talented or capable because I cannot recall a single achievement or deed attributed to you that might allow me to remember who you are.

05:55 Lord Píngyuán continued, you know, people of talent are like an awl or a sharp leather punch that's placed inside a cloth sack. Their talent and ability is like the pointed end of that sharp tool. It will always punch through the fabric and reveal itself.

CHINESE SAYINGS BOOK 2
EPISODE 28

06:13 | Mao Sui said while that may be true, he was like that sharp pointed awl and that had Lord Píngyuán given him a chance and placed him inside that bag, by now he would have seen that he, Mao Sui, was no ordinary rank and file member among his retainers.

06:31 | Máo Suì succeeded in convincing Lord Píngyuán to select him and now with all twenty men in place, they went down to the Chǔ capital to meet with the king and line up his support to help break this siege of Hándān by the Qín army.

06:47 | When Lord Píngyuán sat across from Chǔ King Kǎoliè, and negotiated with him all morning and all afternoon, the king kept shaking his head and refused to consider any kind of alliance, temporary or otherwise. He rebuffed all the entreaties of this envoy from Zhào state and insisted Chǔ would not take part in this military action against Qín.

07:13 | When all appeared lost and with King Kǎoliè not giving Lord Píngyuán any face, it was looking like they were all going to return to Zhào empty-handed. And then from out of the shadows came a strong voice, boldly admonishing the king of Chǔ and asking him what's so difficult about coming to a decision about a matter such as this. And when King Kǎoliè of Chǔ heard this, he asked Lord Píngyuán, who is this guy, speaking out of turn, daring to interrupt. Lord Píngyuán introduced Máo Suì and said he was one of his gang.

CHINESE SAYINGS BOOK 2
EPISODE 28

07:50 | Máo Suì, seeing this whole negotiation going nowhere, approached the King of Chǔ who was aghast at such a breach in protocol. Máo Suì put his hand on the hilt of his sword and said you're only acting so obstinate because you're the king of Chǔ, surrounded by guards. You use your power here to push us around and don't show respect to my lord, Píngyuán.

08:13 | Right now I can pull my sword and decapitate you. King Kǎoliè told Máo Suì that he had his attention. Máo Suì explained plainly that Qín was no friend of Chǔ and had defeated them and had even taken their capital in 278 BC. They remained a threat to Chǔ that got more palpable every day. He asked why on earth given the current situation would Chǔ not come to the aid of Zhào and help break this siege of Hándān. He pleaded with the King to see how this matter was quite simple. Chǔ gets to enjoy some revenge for what Qin had done to them, and at the same time, together with Zhào, they put up a united front against their mutual antagonizer.

09:00 | And after speaking up so forcefully, yet convincingly, like he did, the king of Chǔ was able to see the light and he agreed to come to the aid of Zhào and join together to push Qín away from Hándān.

09:14 | After Lord Píngyuán returned to Zhào, even though a week ago he had no idea who he was, even though he was in his organization for three years. But now he treated Máo Suì as an honored guest. And as Sima Qian wrote in the Shǐjì, Lord Píngyuán said, "Máo xiānshēng

CHINESE SAYINGS BOOK 2
EPISODE 28

yīzhì Chǔ, Chǔ wáng jiù bù gǎn xiǎokàn Zhào Guó. " 毛先生一至楚，楚王就不敢小看赵国。As soon as Mr. Máo arrived in Chǔ, the king of Chǔ did not dare to look down on Zhào.

09:44 And thanks to Máo Suì's exhortations, the Chǔ King indeed came to Zhào's defense. And along with forces sent from Wèi State, Qin was overwhelmed and had to retreat. And thus the siege of the Zhào capital, Hándān, was broken.

10:01 Máo Suì was sort of a one-hit wonder and there's very little if anything else mentioned about him beyond this walk-on role he played in assisting his lord Píngyuán Jūn at a most critical hour. He had boldly volunteered himself as worthy to be among these twenty retainers selected for this mission. And despite Lord Píngyuán's reservations concerning Máo Suì's abilities, when the moment came to shine, Mao Sui rose to the occasion.

10:33 In contemporary usage, Máo Suì Zì Jiàn is often used to encourage proactive and self-confident behavior, especially in situations where one believes they can make a positive impact or contribution. It conveys the idea of stepping up and taking the initiative, and showcasing one's abilities without waiting for others to recognize them.

10:57 It sometimes happen when, in public, or in one's place of employment, or like Máo Suì, when serving your nation, in desperate times when a champion is needed, you volunteer your services and then go on to make all the difference in overcoming the challenge of the moment and assist in achieving whatever the objective is.

11:18 So that's the tale of Máo Suì. He wasn't anyone of consequence, but when the time came, he wasn't afraid to volunteer at a crucial moment, and went on to show he had what it took to solve the crisis or problem at hand. Máo Suì Zì Jiàn. A good one to use. Local, state and national volunteers, they are among the most noble. Let's all keep Máo Suì in the back of our mind.

11:45 Okay, that's gonna be it. So until the next time damas y caballeros, this is Laszlo Montgomery signing off from Santa Monica, California wishing you all my very best and like Máo Suì did to King Kǎoliè, exhorting you to come back next time for another exciting episode of the Chinese Sayings Podcast.

Chinese Sayings Book 2
Episode 29

BE LIKE KONG RONG

孔融让梨—Kǒng Róng Ràng Lí

TRANSCRIPT

00:00 | Hey everyone, Laszlo Montgomery here. Thanks for tuning in to the Chinese Sayings Podcast. Today we have a short one. In fact, in all the years of this educational family program, this just may be the shortest one ever.

00:16 | But that doesn't diminish the lesson it teaches. All of us, all over the world, grew up with our own versions of this chéngyǔ, Kǒng Róng Ràng Lí.

00:27 | This one hearkens back to my younger days growing up in Chicago and reading Highlights Magazine, that popular American children's periodical that first came out in 1946. Aside from all the educational stories and features, Highlights also included moral lessons that were conveyed through the comic strip "Goofus and Gallant."

00:51 | Those were two brothers. One was a model child in every way, thoughtful, selfless, mature kind, generous, and always thinking of others. That was Gallant. His brother

CHINESE SAYINGS BOOK 2
EPISODE 29

Goofus, he was just the opposite. And in every issue the moral lessons learned through these two brothers actions taught me and millions of other young'ns over the years.

01:16 Well, in China, they didn't have Goofus and Gallant but they did offer up the same moral lessons, which kind of shows how humanity and human decency is universal. And this chengyu I am sure, was hammered into the minds of many children growing up in China and Greater China.

01:36 To teach all the young'ns growing up, whenever their parents saw them straying from these virtues, or displaying selfish behavior, they'd make sure to tell their kids to be like Kǒng Róng. He's the star of our Chinese Saying today.

01:52 Kǒng Róng Ràng Lí.

01:55 His name was Kǒng Róng.

01:58 Ràng means to give way, to give ground, yield, give up and to offer, and to allow.

02:05 And a lí is a pear. The fruit.

02:09 Kǒng Róng gives up the pear. Hard to say what that means without having had this story pounded into you during your childhood.

02:18 This story may be a fable but Kǒng Róng, he was a real

CHINESE SAYINGS BOOK 2
EPISODE 29

person. Has his own Wikipedia page and everything. He lived during the Eastern Han between the years 153 and 208. He was a famous literatus and court official as well a twentieth-generation descendant of Confucius, who he shared a surname with. Kǒng Róng was also one of the Seven Scholars of the Jiàn'ān Period, the Jiàn'ān Qīzǐ 建安七子 whose poetry was highly regarded in its day and throughout Chinese history.

02:54 Scholar and upright official he may have been, but Kǒng Róng lived during dangerous times, those raucous years during the last decades of the Hàn Dynasty when Cáo Cāo, Yuán Shào 袁绍, Dǒng Zhuó 董卓 and others were contending to take over the leadership of China from the rotting and decrepit Eastern Hàn.

03:18 Kǒng Róng was an outspoken critic of Cáo Cāo, whose policies he always had something unflattering to say about. And he let it all hang out and feared not any retribution from this unpredictable warlord. He spoke up both to Cáo Cāo's face and behind his back. And one day he went a little bit too far with his critique of Cáo Cāo's leadership and an outraged Cáo Cāo decided to act. He not only had Kǒng Róng executed, he also killed his whole family. Despite his untimely death, Kǒng Róng lived on both in the poems that he left behind and in the following story from his younger days.

04:01 This tale comes from multiple sources. It was first recorded in the New History of the Tales of the World, the Shì Shuō Xīnyǔ 世说新语, written in the beginning of the Northern and Southern Dynasties. This volume was a collection of recordings of the words and deeds of famous people up to that period in the 5th century. It's not technically a 'history', since it does not follow the strict generic conventions required of a history, so this work is classified as a 小说 or fiction.

04:35 It goes like this: When Kǒng Róng was about four years old, he and his five elder brothers and one younger brother were offered a bowl of pears to share. Kǒng Róng was handed the bowl of fruit first and told to take one and offer the rest to his siblings. He stuck his little hand in the bowl and pulled out the smallest pear. Then he handed the bowl to his brothers who each selected the remaining larger sized pears.

05:02 The adults around him saw this and asked, "Why did you give away all the largest pears?" Kǒng Róng replied, "I am the smallest, so by rights I should have the smallest pear."

05:13 His father asked him, but what of your younger brother? He's younger than you, yet you handed him a larger pear. Shouldn't you have handed him the smallest pear? Kǒng Róng replied, He is younger than me and as his elder brother I should look out for him.

05:29 Everyone exclaimed at his precocity and predicted great things for him in the future. So, Kǒng Róng Ràng Lí, Kǒng Róng gives up a pear. Even to this day this fable is taught to children and shows that one is never too young to start practicing virtue, wisdom, and maturity.

CHINESE SAYINGS BOOK 2
EPISODE 29

05:49 So, Kǒng Róng Ràng Lí, this story of Kǒng Róng and the pears became so famous and well-cited that, by the Song dynasty, centuries after Kǒng Róng's lived, it was included in the Three-Character Classic or Sānzìjīng 三字经, a work written in easily-memorizable three-character sentences that was used to teach children literacy and the basic Confucian principles.

06:17 The 三字经 depiction of the incident goes: 融四岁，能让梨。弟于长，宜先知. Róng sì suì, néng ràng lí. Dì yú zhǎng. Yí xiān zhī. 'When Kǒng Róng was four years old, he knew to save the biggest pears for his elder brothers. It is good to know early on the relationships between elder and younger brothers.'

06:40 So that's the story of Kǒng Róng, a renowned writer in the Confucian tradition from two thousand years ago. He was celebrated for his poetry but better remembered for this chéngyǔ: Kǒng Róng Ràng Lí.

06:56 Okay, that's it ladies and gentlemans, this is Laszlo Montgomery once again signing off from Los Angeles. Do consider coming back again next time for another exciting episode of the Chinese Sayings Podcast.

Chinese Sayings Book 2
Episode 30

OWNED!

骄兵必败—Jiāo Bīng Bì Bài

TRANSCRIPT

00:00 | Hey everyone, greetings once again from the Chinese Sayings Podcast. This is your host Laszlo Montgomery and I have another good one for you. I say that all the time, don't I? It's not like I'm gonna go looking for any nothing-special chengyu's.

00:15 | Today we look at Jiāo Bīng Bì Bài. It comes to us from the Hàn Shū, the Book of Han. Most of you will remember the Bān Family of historiographers. The illustrious father Bān Biāo 班彪, and his son and daughter Bān Gù and Bān Zhāo 班昭. And let us not forget their heroic brother, the explorer, diplomat and military great, Bān Chāo 班超 who brought the Western Region, today's Xīnjiāng Province, into the Hàn Dynasty orbit.

00:53 | One of the stars of our chengyu for this time is Hàn Emperor Xuān. You all remember him from past CHP episodes and the chengyu from Season 3 Episode 6, Bǎiwén Bùrú yījiàn 百闻不如一见, seeing is believing. You can hear about a place a hundred times but that

CHINESE SAYINGS BOOK 2
EPISODE 30

	takes a back seat to actually seeing it with your own eyes.
01:16	King Xuān of Hàn is back, so we know this story took place between 91-48 BC. But before we get to the story, let's see what characters make up Jiāo Bīng Bì Bài.
01:30	Jiāo means proud, arrogant, or conceited.
01:33	Bīng means troops or an army.
01:36	Bì means certainly, surely, or must.
01:40	And Bài means to defeat or be defeated.
01:43	Jiāo Bīng Bì Bài. Arrogant troops must be defeated. Well, this is one of those that says what it means. If you hear it, even without knowing the story behind it, you can already figure out what the idiom is getting at.
02:00	But if you do know the story, it takes these four characters and brings them to life and injects some history and Chinese culture into the four syllables.
02:11	So as I said, this one comes from The Book of Hàn, completed in 111 A.D. This is one of the Twenty-Four Official Histories that tells all the goings on that happened in the Western Hàn and the Wáng Mǎng interregnum up to 23 A.D.
02:27	During the Han dynasty, there were frequent skirmishes happening on China's western borders and Chinese were

CHINESE SAYINGS BOOK 2
EPISODE 30

constantly harried and set upon by Xiōngnú infiltrators from the north. One such conflict had occurred in 68 B.C., when the Han army occupied the small border kingdom of Jūshī 车师. All of this, let me mention, has been presented in the CHP History of Xinjiang series. If you never checked it out, I encourage you to suffer through all 12 episodes. This story is included.

03:03   The king of Jūshī, in a panic from seeing all these Han soldiers heading his way, appealed for urgent help from the Xiōngnú. He tried but none of the soldiers sent by the Xiōngnú arrived in time. Left with no other option, the king of Jūshī surrendered to the Hàn forces.

03:22   After the battle, the Hàn commander, Zhèng Jí 郑吉, left an occupying garrison of only three hundred soldiers at Jūshī, and returned eastward with his main force further within the Chinese border.

03:35   As soon as the Xiōngnú learned that the Han main army had retreated, they sent out an invasion force to occupy Jūshī. Zhèng Jí turned heels and hurriedly returned to reinforce his garrison. But the Xiōngnú invasion force was so large that they were easily able to surround both the garrison and Zhèng Jí's reinforcement troops. As a last resort, Zhèng Jí sent word to the Han imperial capital for help.

04:03   When he received Zhèng Jí's plea for help, Emperor Xuān of Han gathered his counselors to discuss the matter. The imperial counselors were divided into two camps. One side thought that if a large Han army were sent out to attack the Xiōngnú right flank, they could easily demolish the entire Xiōngnú force. This would make them think twice about ever attacking inside China's borders again.

04:28 However, the wise and capable prime minister, Wèi Xiàng 魏相, scoffed at this idea. He wrote a memorial to Emperor Xuān explaining his own point of view. He wrote:

04:40 "In recent years, the Xiōngnú have not attacked our own border regions. In these western regions, our citizens live in conditions of utmost poverty. They have no cloth to weave and dress themselves in sheepskins and dog skins. They have no grain to eat and thus eat the seeds of grass. How can we impose more hardship on them for the sake of occupying and controlling Jūshī, an insignificant mere micro-kingdom?"

05:10 He continued, "Furthermore, there is much to occupy our attention within our own nation. Not only are we plagued by natural disasters, there is human misbehavior, as well. Serious reform is needed among the ranks of the court officials, and criminal behavior is increasing within the populace. The imperial court ought not waste its energy on border skirmishes with the Xiōngnú. but should instead strengthen itself from within by initiating legal and bureaucratic reforms.

05:40 "Furthermore, if we send out a huge force to attack the Xiōngnú, even if we win, the consequences will be severe. Nothing good comes of gratuitous displays of

CHINESE SAYINGS BOOK 2
EPISODE 30

force from a country whose strength of population and arms is already self-evident. Such an army is nothing but an arrogant, tyrannical army. An arrogant, tyrannical army is doomed to failure."

06:05 That's right, he said it. Jiāo Bīng Bì Bài. Arrogant soldiers are certain to be defeated. In English we might say, "Pride goes before a fall." That's a less martial version of this chengyu.

06:18 So well-reasoned was this memorial that Emperor Xuān followed Wèi Xiàng's suggested course of action immediately.

06:25 Jiāo Bīng Bì Bài. Arrogant soldiers are certain to be defeated. President George Bush shoulda heeded these words before launching the Second Iraq War and invading Afghanistan. And President Putin? Same thing Jiāo Bīng Bì Bài. His special military operation, though not defeated yet, shoulda pondered the meaning behind Jiāo Bīng Bì Bài.

06:53 Napoleon and Hitler too, someone shoulda told them Jiāo Bīng Bì Bài in 1812 and 1941 before they invaded Russia. And again the French were Jiāo Bīng Bì Bài and got their rear ends handed to them at Dien Bien Phu in 1954. The Brits? General Burgoyne was absolutely certain in 1777 that he had the American colonists in the bag. But at Saratoga, he had to surrender. Jiāo Bīng Bì Bài. A good one for us all, but mostly for the leaders of nations always trying to pick on those they perceive as easy meat.

CHINESE SAYINGS BOOK 2
EPISODE 30

07:35 Okay, that's gonna be it from me little beauties. Don't forget, if you'd like to throw a few rubles or shillings in my tin cup and help me support my ten cats n' kittens who are all living off my generosity and weakness for all things feline, feel free to donate. You can hit me up too with a Super Thanks at my YouTube channel, Buy Me a Coffee, get a prescription to my Patreon or CHP Premium, or donate via various other ways. Go to teacup.media and click on support where you can view the plethora of options. I thank you.

08:09 Okay, this is Laszlo Montgomery signing off from Los Angeles, as usual. Two more to go before we bring the curtain down on this 9th season of the CSP. Come on back next time, if you please, and join me once more for another exciting episode of the Chinese Sayings Podcast.

Chinese Sayings Book 2
Episode 31

FIRST STRIKE

先发制人—Xiān Fā Zhì Rén

TRANSCRIPT

00:00 | Good evening everyone, all appreciators and lovers of Chinese chéngyǔ sayings. Laszlo Montgomery here with one more for your expanding collezione.

00:11 | Today we're pulling out a couple of the heavy hitters. We have the mighty Xiàng Liáng and his even mightier nephew, Xiàng Yǔ, appearing.

00:20 | This is the 3rd time Xiàng Yǔ's showing up in a CSP episode. We first encountered him in Season 2 with Sì Miàn Chǔ Gē 四面楚歌. And again in Season 3 with Pò Fǔ Chén Zhōu 破釜沉舟 and last time in Season 7 with Jiè Zhù Dài Chóu 借箸代筹.

00:38 | And he's back again. And why not. This Chinese Saying comes from the definitive source for all things Xiàng Yǔ, the Record of the Grand Historian, the chapter entitled Xiàng Yǔ Běnjì 项羽本纪.

CHINESE SAYINGS BOOK 2
EPISODE 31

00:51 | Today we look at Xiān Fā Zhì Rén. Let's see what this means.

00:58 | Xiān, as an adverb, means earlier, before, first or in advance.

01:04 | Fā means to send, issue, launch, emit and a whole bunch of other definitions.

01:12 | Zhì in this case means to control or regulate.

01:15 | And rén means a person.

01:8 | And when you string them together, first launch control person, though I'm betting Sima Qian meant a man when he said person.

01:27 | The star of this chengyu isn't Xiàng Yǔ. Instead it's his uncle Xiàng Liáng 项梁. And as the story begins, the the Dàzéxiāng Uprising was sending shockwaves through the Qín Empire. All that sordid stuff was going down with Qín Èrshì 秦二世, Zhào Gāo 赵高, and Lǐ Sī 李斯.

01:46 | We remember the Dàzéxiāng Uprising and the two colorful characters who led it. Chén Shèng 陈胜 and Wú Guǎng 吴广. In a lot of history books, it's even called the Chén Shèng Wú Guǎng Uprising. It lasted from August 209 to January 208 BC.

02:03 | Some of you, who really pay attention, remember Chén Shèng from the Season 3 episode Hóng hú zhī zhì 鸿鹄之志. How can a sparrow comprehend the ambition of a

CHINESE SAYINGS BOOK 2
EPISODE 31

swan? Chén Shèng was just a commoner who was also a man of great ambition. And though his uprising failed in its mission, he did go down in history as the one who lit the fuse that led to the bloody end of the Qín Dynasty.

02:31 So while this whole uprising was going on, Xiàng Liáng, a major guy at the time because of his oversized reputation. He got written out of the script very early on. And had he not died so young at Dìngtáo 定陶 in 208 BC, the successor dynasty to the Qín might very well have been the Chǔ Dynasty instead of the Hàn.

02:54 Xiàng Yǔ was a mighty warrior. He learned from his uncle Xiàng Liáng. And lest we forget what Xiàng Yǔ did to avenge his uncle's death after vanquishing the Qin at Jùlù 巨鹿 in 207 BC, 200,000 Qin soldiers buried alive on his orders.

03:15 One day the governor of the Kuàijī Commandery 会稽郡, a man named Yīn Tōng 殷通, invited Xiàng Liáng to call on him and to discuss the latest situation regarding the viability of the Qín and what the future portended. Kuàijī, by the way is an ancient name for the great city of Sūzhōu.

03:34 So while he was sitting with Yīn Tōng at the Kuàijī Commandery they began exchanging news and viewpoints. Yīn Tōng revealed to Xiàng Liáng that he believed with so many people rising up in Jiāngxī and elsewhere north of the Yangzi River, it's Heaven's will that the Qín Dynasty shall fall. He further said that he was going to start a rebellion himself and overthrow the Qín. And according to Sīmǎ Qiān, here is where Yīn Tōng said to Xiàng Liáng, Xiānfā Zhìrén.

04:06 The first one to send troops will be the one to control the people. In other words, the one who takes a preemptive strike, xiānfā, can gain the initiative to control their opponents and then the people. Then in so many words he asked Xiàng Liáng, are you in or you out?

04:27 During the conversation Xiàng Liáng studied Yīn Tōng closely and in the short span of their discussion, he knew Yīn Tōng was weak, incompetent, and hardly qualified to lead a rebellion against the Qín. There was no way he could take orders from a man like the governor. After retiring for a moment to consider, Xiàng Liáng consulted with his nephew. He told Xiàng Yǔ to take his sword, go in there and kill Yīn Tōng and decapitate him.

04:59 And right here is where Xiàng Liáng, with Xiàng Yǔ at his side, seized control of the Kuàijī Commandery and rallied 8,000 men to his side. And carrying the head of Yīn Tōng in his hand for the gathered crowd to see, Xiàng Liáng proclaimed himself the new governor of Kuàijī and appointed his nephew Xiàng Yǔ as a general. And these soldiers who joined him on that day became the core of Xiàng Liáng and later Xiàng Yǔ's army.

05:29 So Xiàng Liáng took these words to heart. Xiānfā Zhìrén. A preemptive strike was necessary to gain control of the people. One needed to strike first to gain the upper hand in battle. And once that's out of the way, they can control and subdue the populace.

CHINESE SAYINGS BOOK 2
EPISODE 31

05:47 | So anytime there's a need to say something to the extent of strike while the iron is hot to achieve your objective, whatever it may be, these are the four words to consider. Xiānfā Zhìrén. The one to take the initiative first will be the one to prevail in the end. Same thing in the unforgiving hand of the market. If you strike first, and get your product out before your competitors, you will seize the day and control the market. You get the main idea. Xiānfā Zhìrén. To launch an attack first in order to be in an advantageous position. To strike first to gain the upper hand.

06:28 | And that, my fine friends, is gonna be that. I thank you all for listening. This is Laszlo Montgomery signing off from Los Angeles, California, entreating you to join me again next time for another exciting episode of the Chinese Sayings Podcast.

ABOUT THE AUTHOR

Laszlo Montgomery is the creator and presenter of the China History Podcast, and other Chinese culture related podcasts. He began his Chinese studies in 1979 at the University of Illinois, and lived in Hong Kong between 1989-1998. He has helped Chinese companies build market share in the US, and in 2010, launched The China History Podcast as a channel to allow a more mass, non-academic audience to enjoy the delights of Chinese history. Originally intended for a US audience, today more than half of the show's listeners are outside the States. Cathay Pacific Airways has carried Laszlo's content on their inflight entertainment system since 2017. Laszlo has spoken frequently at universities and high schools about his love for Chinese history and culture.

www.ingramcontent.com/pod-product-compliance
Lightning Source LLC
LaVergne TN
LVHW061610070526
838199LV00078B/7228